THE LIVING GOD

THE LIVING GOD

*Christian Belief
for Everyone*

Book 2

THE LIVING GOD

Alister McGrath

First published in Great Britain in 2013

Society for Promoting Christian Knowledge
36 Causton Street
London SW1P 4ST
www.spckpublishing.co.uk

British Library Cataloguing-in-Publication Data
A catalogue record for this book is available from the British Library

ISBN 978–0–281–06835–7
eBook ISBN 978–0–281–06836–4

Typeset by Graphicraft Limited, Hong Kong
Manufacture managed by Jellyfish
First printed in Great Britain by CPI Group
Subsequently digitally printed in Great Britain

eBook by Graphicraft Limited, Hong Kong

Produced on paper from sustainable forests

Contents

THE LIVING GOD

THE LIVING GOD

Introduction

Faith and the Creeds, the first volume in the Christian Belief for Everyone series, explored why we need creeds and how they enrich our vision of the Christian faith and life. In this second volume we move on to consider what Christians mean when they speak about God.

The little word 'God' packs a big punch. The creeds cannot hope, and do not intend, to tell us what it *feels* like to believe and trust in God, nor the difference that this may make to the way we live. They do not convey a sense of the glory of God, so central to Christian worship and adoration. But they do provide us with a framework for putting and holding together our own understanding of the nature of God.

Shortly after I had learned to read and write at school, our teacher told us we were going to try a new game. It was about telling a story. Taking a piece of chalk, she wrote a few sentences on the blackboard. They introduced us to two characters – I think they were called Janet and John – and gave us some background about their homes and characters. After making sure we had absorbed this basic information, our teacher chalked up another sentence that went something like this: 'One day, Janet and John had an adventure!' 'Now,' she said, 'you have half an hour to write about what happened next.' Having started the story for us, she was encouraging us to finish it. I can't remember exactly what I wrote, but I do recall having to ask my parents what the phrase 'an overactive imagination' meant when I returned home later that day.

In a similar way, the creeds offer us some basic statements about God and invite us to add colour and detail. Gradually, our personal insights are supplemented by material from books we've read, sermons we've found valuable, conversations we've had – and indeed from the rich quarry of Christian history and experience that's ours to mine.

'I believe in God, the Father Almighty, Creator of Heaven and Earth.' This mere handful of words is the starting point for our journey of exploration. We learn that the foundation of our faith, the anchor of our souls is God. But the word 'God' needs to be opened up. Which God do we mean?

The creeds respond by stating that this God is the 'Father'. The God that lies at the heart of the Christian faith is the same God who was known and trusted by Jesus of Nazareth. To trust Jesus is to trust 'the God and Father of our Lord Jesus Christ' (Ephesians 1.3).

Thinking about God as Father prompts us to consider the rich imagery that both the Old and New Testaments use to help us picture God. Images such as 'shepherd', 'rock', 'mother' and 'friend' enable us to put into words things we know about God that would otherwise be difficult to express.

The creeds then tell us that God is 'almighty'. The sense of the Greek term that lies behind this statement is really, 'the one who rules everything' or perhaps even, 'the one who upholds everything'. This naturally leads us to reflect on God as the creator of the world.

Yet there is another concept of God that neither the Apostles' Creed nor the Nicene Creed makes explicit. It relates to the Trinity, which for many Christians is a perplexing idea, amounting to little more than some baffling celestial mathematics.

Why make a simple faith unnecessarily complicated? In Chapter 5, 'Mystery or muddle? The Trinity', I try to explain why Christians came to the conclusion that they had to speak of God in this way, and why it actually makes a lot of sense to do so.

Like the first volume in the series, this book is based on sermons I preached over a number of years, and I take the greatest pleasure in dedicating it to the people of the Shill Valley and Broadshire benefice in west Oxfordshire, consisting of the churches in the Cotswold villages of Alvescot, Black Bourton, Broadwell, Broughton Poggs, Filkins, Holwell, Kelmscott, Kencot, Langford, Little Faringdon, Shilton and Westwell.

Alister McGrath

1

Which God are we talking about?

It was prize-giving day at my school. As usual a distinguished visitor had been invited to lend a little dignity to what might otherwise be a rather dull occasion, and before presenting the prizes he was invited to give a short address. The visitor was introduced in glowing terms as one of the greatest thinkers and writers Ireland had ever produced. This giant had descended from Olympus to talk to us! What a privilege! Rarely have I experienced such a sense of anticipation – my friends and I were on the edges of our seats with excitement.

Then he began to speak.

After about ten seconds, we realized we were in the presence of possibly the dullest person in Ireland. The speech probably lasted only ten minutes but it seemed like an eternity. My friends started passing notes to each other. Others held their heads in their hands or studied their watches in the hope that this would somehow make time pass quicker. To my relief I cannot remember the name of the speaker – like the speech itself it was best forgotten. The real problem was that there was a massive disconnection between what we were led to expect and what we actually experienced. The speech was lousy, probably thrown together hastily on the back of an envelope; but it was made even worse by our expectation that it would be brilliant.

Perhaps we approach the creeds with similarly unrealistic expectations. Do we anticipate a heart-stirring affirmation of the glorious riches of the Christian faith? If so we may be rather disappointed to find that there is a complete lack of dramatic build-up – and certainly no fanfare of trumpets – before the rather curt opening, 'I believe in God'. As a statement it sounds about as exciting as, 'I think it's Saturday'.

It's important to understand what the creeds are trying to do. They are not meant to convince outsiders of the truth of Christianity, nor give an exhaustive account of what Christians believe. Neither are they accounts of God's superlative beauty and radiance, designed to attract the attention of curious bystanders. They were written by our forebears to help us enumerate the basic themes of our faith, allow us to savour them in their fullness and ensure we leave nothing out. As we saw in the previous volume in this series, the creeds are but sketch maps of the beautiful landscape of the Christian faith.

So who are the creeds talking about when they speak of God? We can forget the 'abstract philosophical idea' so beloved of armchair philosophers, and Homer's grudge-bearing Greek Olympian deities, out to settle scores after being snubbed by upstart mortals or outwitted by other gods! The creeds bear witness to the God who is made known in and through Jesus of Nazareth, and they invite us to linger, ponder and savour all we know about that God. They encourage us to go deeper and further into the mystery of things not yet fully revealed.

The starting point for any sensible thinking about God is to realize that the human mind just isn't big enough to cope with such a concept. It's like trying to pack the Alps into a suitcase or the Niagara Falls into a coffee mug. How can the little word 'God' do justice to the magnificent reality to which it points? We can no more reduce God to words than we can take hold of the smoke of a candle that's just been blown out, or capture sunbeams in a glass jar.

To use a more formal way of speaking, we can't *comprehend* God – human reason is simply not capable of grasping God in full. It may try to prove and to define things about God, only to discover that what it has defined and proved bears little relationship to the 'God and Father of our Lord Jesus Christ'. So while it's great fun to explore human ideas about God, in the end we need to pay God the ultimate compliment. *You* tell us who you are! *You* tell us what you're like! *You* approach *us* . . .

Some hear God calling them by name in the night. Like Samuel (see 1 Samuel 3) – they perceive a voice amid the darkness of the world and feel an urge to discover who is speaking and where this call might take them. Others read the Bible and sense they are being addressed directly by a person behind or within the text. For some, God is the one hidden in the beauty of a glorious sunset, in the breathtaking grandeur of a distant mountain range; for others, a living reality with whom they come into contact in prayer and worship. And for some, of course, God is all of these – and more.

Let's look at one person's encounter with God in more detail. The German writer Jürgen Moltmann (b. 1926), seen by many as one of the finest theologians of the twentieth century, developed a deep understanding of the way Christianity can speak into situations of suffering and pain. He once told me about how he came to faith,[1] his secular 'enlightened' family in Hamburg having had no interest in spiritual matters. Moltmann was drafted into military service in 1944 and captured by British troops in the final year of the Second World War. While a prisoner in Scotland, a well-meaning chaplain gave him a Bible, which he started to read. Moltmann found Psalm 39 spoke to him of someone who felt far from God but yearned to return, and he began to hear an echo of the Psalm's themes deep within his own soul – 'It called that soul back to God.'[2]

Moltmann was especially moved by the passion story in Mark's Gospel, which revealed Jesus of Nazareth as the 'companion on the way, who goes with you through this "valley of the shadow of death", the fellow-sufferer who carries you, with your suffering'.[3] He found his life changing as he 'was surely but slowly seized by a great hope for the resurrection'.

Moltmann's experience reminds us of the power of God to speak to people through the text of Scripture. Like Samuel, Moltmann heard the voice of God calling him – and responded. Yet the remainder of his professional career was spent trying to deepen his grasp and understanding of this God he discovered in a prison camp – which brings us to the next important question: how do we get to know about God?

How do we know about God?

The God the creeds are speaking about is not some abstract entity but a living reality who engages, calls and loves us and whom we are invited to know and trust. As C. S. Lewis pointed out, God is not just some impersonal 'force' behind the universe. God may well be *more* than personal but is certainly not less. Our living, loving God stands at the heart of the biblical narrative and the Christian faith – the God of Abraham, Isaac and Jacob, and the God of Jesus Christ.

In 2007, in Washington, I was debating with Christopher Hitchens, one of the most vociferous advocates of atheism. We had time to exchange a few words before the debate, and I suggested that his rejection of God fell into the same logical landscape as my acceptance of God – somewhere between certainty and doubt. Hitchens would have none of this. He *knew* his atheism was right and had no need to prove it to irritating people like me. After all, would any sane person want to follow a divine despot who behaved like a North Korean dictator? Well, I didn't, and told him so. The God I believed in, I explained, was nothing like the one he didn't believe in. I also expressed surprise that he had chosen the leader of North Korea – one of the last remaining strongholds of dogmatic political atheism – as an analogy for God! Surely it was self-defeating to have to use such a nasty atheist as a model?

It was an interesting discussion and made me wonder if Hitchens might actually have preferred God to exist. He seemed to want to scapegoat God for everything that was wrong with the world. But if the central belief of atheism is true, the spotlight of blame shifts relentlessly on to human beings. If there is no God, then responsibility for messing things up lies squarely with us! Yet my most important memory of that conversation concerned how everything depends on having a right understanding of God. All too often, 'I don't believe in God' really means, 'I don't believe in *a certain kind of God*'. Lots of people adopt or invent a particular idea of God – and then reject it because they don't like it. But what if we get God wrong? What if we reject a caricature of the real thing? How can we know what God is *really* like?

With regard to this last question, Christians have always realized they're in need of divine help! We can only get so far 'under our own steam', as C. S. Lewis put it. Our deepest intuitions may point us in the right direction but they won't take us a particularly long way and can easily lead to an inadequate or distorted vision of God. We may believe God is the true goal of human reason but all too easily end up trapped with what Lewis called a 'glib and shallow rationalism' that limits our vision. We may believe God is the ultimate desire of the human heart, but find our desires getting attached to lesser goals, which then become our gods. First we lose our bearings; then we get sidetracked; then we get lost. Happily, God is aware that we often end up muddled and confused and offers help in the form of 'revelation'. Who is God? And what is God like? Well, God *tells* us and God *shows* us.

Where dictionaries offer vague definitions of 'a supreme being', Christianity tells of a God who enters history and encounters people – such as Abraham, who met God and found his life was transformed as a result. Abraham, Isaac, Jacob and Moses *tell* us what this God was like, and at the heart of the Christian faith lies the story of Jesus of Nazareth, whose words and deeds disclose the will and character of God. Jesus *shows* us what God is like. Christianity points to people God encountered, to events in which God was discerned and experienced, and to images that illuminate God's character. Let us explore each of these points further.

Forebears of faith: Abraham, Isaac and Jacob

Everyone loves exploring their family history. Sometimes it's just because we enjoy finding out things about the past. I was fascinated to discover that a relative had been one of the last people to get to safety from the Cunard liner *Lusitania* after it was torpedoed by a German submarine in 1915. Another was a British Cavalry officer who took part in the famous Charge of the Light Brigade in 1854 – and survived to tell the tale.

Yet historical interest aside, exploring our family's roots is a way of enriching our own story and setting it in a deeper context. As we uncover a web of interconnecting stories, linked to many others over the spread of history, we may find – though sadly not in my case – that we're related to someone really important. Knowing the family history brings a new depth to our understanding of our own identity and significance.

Christians believe in the 'God of Abraham, of Isaac, and of Jacob' (Exodus 3.16). Faith stretches back to the dawn of civilization. We hold hands with millions who have known and loved our God and passed their wisdom on to us. When we read of the great biblical figures – people to whom we are linked by the bond of faith – we are absorbing our own family history. The Christian community tells a story it believes both to be rooted in the bedrock of history and to offer a 'big picture' that makes sense of what we see around us and experience within.

As the curtain of history lifts, we come to the first great story of faith – the calling of Abraham, which has parallels with Jesus' calling of the first disciples by the shore of Lake Galilee centuries later. In their encounter in the desert:

> the LORD said to Abram, 'Go from your country and your kindred and your father's house to the land that I will show you. I will make of you a great nation, and I will bless you, and make your name great, so that you will be a blessing.'
>
> (Genesis 12.1–2)

This passage has two striking features. First, it combines promise and task: God asks Abraham to do something and promises him blessing and support as he does it. We find this twofold pattern throughout the biblical narrative. For example, in the 'Great Commission' Jesus of Nazareth charges his disciples to 'make disciples of all nations', while at the same time promising that he will be with them always, even to the end of time (Matthew 28.17–20).

The second striking feature is the name used to designate God – 'the LORD'. This is the widely accepted way of representing the name of the covenant God of Israel, and appears nearly 7,000 times in the Old Testament. The four Hebrew letters YHWH (translated 'LORD') are sometimes written as 'Yahweh' (or in older English translations as 'Jehovah'). This is not a generic word for God but a proper name, referring specifically to the God who called Abraham and began to build a people who would reach out to the world.

The word 'god' would not have conveyed much information in the Ancient Near East – the religious worlds of ancient Egypt, Babylonia and Anatolia were cluttered with deities. Which one did you mean? Which god are you talking about? Israel increasingly came to describe its own special god with reference to the acts of God: this was the God who called Abraham, Isaac and Jacob; this was the God who led Israel out of captivity in Egypt into the Promised Land. Reciting such acts was seen as a way of making sure everyone understood who you were talking about. The Psalms, for example, regularly refer to the acts of God in history.

In the sight of their ancestors [God] worked marvels
    in the land of Egypt, in the fields of Zoan.
He divided the sea and let them pass through it,
    and made the waters stand like a heap.
In the daytime he led them with a cloud,
    and all night long with a fiery light.
He split rocks open in the wilderness,
    and gave them drink abundantly as from the deep.
                         (Psalm 78.12–15)

Question: who is God? Answer: whoever brought us out of
Egypt and into the Promised Land.

Yet for Christians the most important answer to that same
question references Jesus of Nazareth. Question: who is
God? Answer: 'the God and Father of our Lord Jesus Christ'
(1 Peter 1.3; see also 1 Corinthians 1.3). Jesus of Nazareth
did rather more than simply talk about God; he showed us
what God is like. Let's look at this in more detail.

The God of Jesus of Nazareth

Don't *tell* them – *show* them! That was the advice I was given
when trying to improve my preaching more than 30 years
ago. My early attempts were not particularly successful. I
remember two people coming up to me after a sermon I
preached in 1980. 'We think you were trying to tell us something very important,' they said, 'but we're still not quite
sure what it was.' I later realized that one of my problems
was that I tried to get across lots of ideas, without giving
appropriate analogies or stories to help them see that these
things made sense.

So what is God like? Some of the finest passages in the
Old Testament tell us about God's graciousness, majesty

and love. God is like a shepherd who journeys with his people, guiding and protecting them. God is like rain in a parched desert, bringing refreshment and new life to our souls. We'll explore some of these images in more detail later.

Yet the New Testament opens up a new way of thinking about God, based on the life, death and resurrection of Jesus of Nazareth. Jesus both *tells* us and *shows* us what God is like. Jesus is the 'image of the invisible God' (Colossians 1.15). He makes God visible and tangible: 'the Word became flesh and lived among us, and we have seen his glory' (John 1.14). Through his words, Jesus teaches us what God is like and how we ought to behave as a result. Yet in his person and actions, Jesus *shows* what God is like.

Theologians use the word 'incarnation' to express this idea that Jesus of Nazareth *embodies* God. God is with us not merely in the sense of being on our side – though that is a rather wonderful idea – but also of standing alongside us, sharing our story and journeying with us. God's commitment to us is expressed in action, not simply in words. God does not speak to us from a distance but comes to where we are in order to meet us. We'll look at why this idea makes sense of the New Testament witness to Jesus of Nazareth in the next volume in the series, *Lord and Saviour: Jesus of Nazareth*, but let's reflect briefly on why it is so important to our thinking about God.

I was invited to give a lecture at a university in Texas. It's a long way from London to Texas and my diary was very full. Sadly, I had to say no, but I mentioned that I could manage to produce a video recording of the lecture to send instead, if that was any use. The conference organizers accepted my suggestion and the recording was duly played at the conference. I had several messages from participants afterwards. They loved the lecture but not the medium. 'It would have been so good to meet you', one wrote. Another commented that I was not really 'present' at the conference, just some kind of 'virtual reality' without embodiment in Texas; a 'projection not a person'.

I knew exactly what they were getting at. We like to see people in the flesh rather than only reading their books or listening to prerecorded talks. Had I been able to attend the conference I would have taken the time and trouble to journey to Texas, which would have expressed my commitment to the audience. I often think about that episode when reflecting on the incarnation. The wonderful truth is that God showed us how much we matter by coming all the way to be with us rather than sending us messages from a safe distance. God's commitment to us is seen, first, in creating us and, second, in coming to dwell among us.

Philosophers might enjoy the logical riddles of wrestling with a divine reality that is immortal, invisible and incomprehensible, as the textbooks put it. But the doctrine of the incarnation asks us to think of a tangible God – the 'word become flesh'. Abstract concepts of God tend to fly out of the window when we find ourselves presented with the imaginatively compelling vision of holiness that is expressed and embodied in the story of Jesus of Nazareth. Here is someone who resists temptations to power and grandeur, who loves the lost and outcast, heals the sick, hates religious pettiness and pedantry, suffers graciously and nobly, forgives his executioners and, finally, lays down his life for his people. The incarnation speaks of a God who is revealed in an accessible and meaningful manner – one who enters, inhabits and changes our fallen and miserable history. We have got lost:

we can find our way home only because God leaves home in order to bring us back.

Some Christians get preoccupied with maintaining their purity and trying to avoid being contaminated by the darkness of the world around them. But the idea of the incarnation is that God chose to enter into this world and to run the risk of being overwhelmed by it. To use the language of C. S. Lewis, the incarnation is about bringing a 'good infection', a cure for the world's ills. In order to offer healing and renewal, the physician had to enter a diseased and disordered world.

This brings us to another central aspect of the Christian understanding about God – that events in history tell us something about the identity and nature of God.

Seeing God in the events of history

Universities are wonderful places for having arguments yet staying friends afterwards. A colleague and I were swapping views on God. He liked the idea of God he found in the writings of the seventeenth-century scientist and philosopher Isaac Newton. I wasn't so sure. We spent a happy half hour exploring the issues while we waited for a visiting lecturer to arrive – his train was late. My friend took the view that God made the world and then left it to its own devices – like a clockmaker constructing and winding up a watch and then letting it go on its own, an idea we'll explore further in Chapter 4. 'But your God doesn't *do* anything!' I protested. 'That's the way I like it!' he replied.

I could understand his position. C. S. Lewis famously resisted believing in God for much the same reason. For Lewis, God would be a burden, compromising his freedom to do what he liked. 'I had always wanted, above all things, not to be "interfered with".'[4] In the end, Lewis felt he was simply running away from reality by continuing to resist God. 'I gave in, and admitted that God was God, and knelt and prayed: perhaps, that night, the most dejected and reluctant convert in all England.'[5] Lewis realized that he had been treating God simply as an idea – only to discover that God was a living reality who was drawing near to him.

Christianity knows a God who is at work in the world, in ways that we do not entirely understand. Sometimes the presence of God seems hidden or veiled, so that it is not immediately obvious – 'now we see in a mirror, dimly' (1 Corinthians 13.12); sometimes it seems so real and tangible that it cannot be ignored.

The people of Israel constantly looked back to a defining moment in their history when they believed that the power and presence of God could not be overlooked – their exodus from slavery in Egypt, through 40 years of wandering in the wilderness, to eventual freedom in the Promised Land. This dramatic story of liberation, for all its human drama, also revealed God's compassion and faithfulness. Generations later, Israel would remember this event and its deeper meaning.

> It was because the LORD loved you and kept the oath that he swore to your ancestors, that the LORD has brought you out with a mighty hand, and redeemed you from the house of slavery, from the hand of Pharaoh king of Egypt. Know therefore that the LORD your God is God, the faithful God who maintains covenant loyalty with those who love him and keep his commandments, to a thousand generations.
>
> (Deuteronomy 7.8–9)

Events need interpretation. We may not immediately grasp the full story or see what's going on beneath the outward appearance. It can be necessary to dig deeper. Britain declared war on Germany in September 1939 and, after an initial 'phoney war' in which nothing very much happened, German armies moved westwards into France, driving all from their path. It seemed that little could stop the German advance. By May 1940, the British Expeditionary Force was surrounded on the beaches of Dunkirk, a French coastal town just across the English Channel from the south-eastern county of Kent. Unless the force could be evacuated by sea, it would be wiped out. A call went out for everyone who owned boats of any kind to sail to Dunkirk, pick up as many soldiers as they could, and bring them home to England.

Now imagine two people standing together on the white cliffs of Dover at some point in late May 1940. Both would see lots of small boats coming and going from the local harbours. The first might think, 'So what? This is the coast. Boats move around all the time there. Nothing important there, surely?'

But the second, knowing that the little boats were engaged in the evacuation of the British Expeditionary Force from Dunkirk, would be aware of a deeper and more significant truth that the first person had missed. The first person just skimmed the surface of reality; the second discerned a deeper truth. As it turned out, the success of the Dunkirk evacuation – hailed as a 'miracle' by Prime Minister Winston Churchill – held the key to further resistance to Adolf Hitler, on which the outcome of the Second World War would ultimately depend.

Let's go back to the exodus from Egypt, one of the great events of the Old Testament. Perhaps the Egyptians saw the departure of the Israelites as a bit of bad luck, the result of a political or military miscalculation. The Israelites however had no doubt about the true significance of what was happening: they were being led out of Egypt by a God who journeyed with them and had promised to be with them and their descendants. Israel had known this God long before the exodus: this great event was seen as the culmination of a long history of mutual commitment between a people and their God – a demonstration of God's faithfulness and power and an assurance of God's presence in the future. The exodus from Egypt was thus understood at a deeper level than a mere migration of people or some kind of historical accident. It was about God acting to liberate Israel from its bondage in Egypt and leading her to a Promised Land.

For Christians, the great events in which the hand of God was to be discerned were the crucifixion and resurrection of Jesus of Nazareth. The resurrection was like a new exodus – a fresh act of divine deliverance that brought hope and freedom to humanity. This time the enemy was not an enslaving nation but an enslaving fear. Through the resurrection, God chose to 'free those who all their lives were held in slavery by the fear of death' (Hebrews 2.15). We shall have more to say about this in our reflections on the significance of Jesus of Nazareth in the next volume, *Lord and Saviour: Jesus of Nazareth*, and on the Christian hope in the final volume of this series, *The Christian Life and Hope*.

Images as windows into God

'A picture is worth a thousand words.' Being able to show someone a picture of a beautiful scene, a complicated piece of machinery or a pet cat goes a long way towards making up for the limitations of human words. So perhaps we should not be surprised that the Bible is rich in analogies: there are many instances of two things that are similar in some way being compared in order to make a difficult concept easier to understand. God, we find, is portrayed in a rich diversity of manners – for example, as a lion and as a shepherd. Dorothy L. Sayers recognized the importance of images to our thinking about God, arguing that we simply cannot do without them.

> No legislation could prevent the making of verbal pictures: God walks in the garden, He stretches out His arm, His voice shakes the cedars, His eyelids try the children of men. To forbid the making of pictures about God would be to forbid thinking about God at all, for man is so made that he has no way to think except in pictures.[6]

The same is true in connection with science. As I mentioned in *Faith and the Creeds*, I was much helped by the great physicist Ernest Rutherford suggesting – back in the 1910s – that we think of atoms as being like miniature solar systems, with electrons like planets orbiting the central nucleus. Now atoms look nothing like this, but it's a helpful way of visualizing them and making sense of some of their properties. Scientists use analogies – or 'models' – a lot to help us understand something much more complicated, but we need to realize that they are not identical with what they're being used to describe.

Let's look at a few biblical images to grasp this point more firmly. Many passages of Scripture speak of God as our 'light' (for example, Psalm 27.1), and this theme is often associated with the celebration of Christmas. We are reminded that in Jesus of Nazareth: 'The true light, which enlightens everyone, was coming into the world' (John 1.9). Why is this image so significant?

First of all, it tells us something about our own situation. It suggests that we are lost, or at least having difficulty finding the way. But there is someone to light up the road ahead of us so we can make the journey home: 'Your word is a lamp to my feet and a light to my path' (Psalm 119.105). The image also suggests that we are unable to perceive the 'big picture' without assistance – a theme we explored in *Faith and the Creeds*. To perceive that we need God's help to see things as they really are is to get to the heart of the Christian understanding of revelation. I remember explaining Christianity's distinctive way of viewing the world to an academic in Melbourne some years ago. 'It was as if someone had turned a light on', he told me afterwards. 'Suddenly, I saw things in a new way. And they made sense for the first time.' Another idea you might find useful is that we have been made with a homing instinct for God, and are drawn to God as a moth is drawn to light.

The second image I want to explore is that of God as a 'rock', which might initially seem a rather unpromising analogy – a rock is barren and lifeless. But as with every analogy, the reader must work out how the image might best be applied and interpreted – and context can be hugely helpful: '[God] alone is my rock and my salvation, my fortress; I shall not be shaken. On God rests my deliverance and my honour; my mighty rock, my refuge is in God' (Psalm 62.6–7).

The interpretation we are to make is that *a rock is a place of stability and security and God is like this, too*. God is a safe place on which we can stand and from which we can see things more clearly. Now there's more to God than this, but it's a great starting point and resonates strongly with both the biblical witness and human experience.

A friend of my family devotedly built up a business in Belfast over many years. By the time I came to know him, it had become more or less his only reason for living. He saw himself as a dedicated and committed businessman; everyone else thought he was a man obsessed who was neglecting his family and friends. His identity and sense of self-worth were totally wrapped up in his work.

Then disaster struck. During one of the riots in Belfast during the early 1970s, the business was torched by a mob and burnt to the ground. Our friend was able to claim compensation but it wasn't enough to allow him to recover, and the business folded. At this point, with everything in which he had invested gone and only memories remaining, it seemed to him that existence had ceased to be meaningful. Devastated and in despair, he considered suicide.

In the end he came to his senses. God, who had been sidelined on the margins of his life, now became its foundation – everything else was shifting sand but God was a rock on which he could rebuild things. The storms of life might batter him but he would no longer be shaken or overwhelmed for he had found the place of safety where he belonged.

The analogy of God as a rock helps us see what really matters in life, but there are many other images we can draw on to gain a deeper and richer vision of God. One of the most familiar and best loved is that of a shepherd (Psalm 23).

A shepherd cares for his sheep, guiding them to food and water and protecting them from attack. He journeys with them as they travel through hostile landscapes. And so we can trust that, even when we pass through the valley of the shadow of death, God is by our side, holding us by the hand. This powerful vision speaks deeply to many as they face challenges and difficulties. It reassures us that we are not on our own in this puzzling and confusing world. There is someone accompanying us as we travel and we can trust we are being led home.

Moving on

In this chapter we have explored two slightly different – but converging – themes. First, we have identified God *relationally*. Christians know and love – as they are in turn known and loved by – the same God known and loved by Abraham and Moses. The Letter to the Hebrews takes great pleasure in providing a long list of faithful men and women from this era, reminding us that, when we feel disheartened or discouraged, we can look to this 'so great a cloud of witnesses' (Hebrews 12.1) who have made the journey of faith before us and entered into the promises that await us, too. And in fact not only do we share their faith but we also have an amplified, enriched vision of it through the coming of Jesus of Nazareth.

Second, we have identified God *functionally* – by considering the difference that God makes to the way we think and live. For Christians, the opening statement of the creed, 'I believe in God', is a joyful declaration that there is meaning in life; that we can find security and stability; that we are known and loved by someone who really matters. We should delight in this to the full!

Yet there is a third way of thinking about God. We have seen how we can reflect on those who knew and loved this God before we did. And we have noted how thinking about

19

what God does enables a deeper appreciation of the difference God makes to us. But alongside these relational and functional approaches there is another that we have yet to explore – a *personal* approach, which focuses on God as someone we can *know* and not just *know about*. We will think about this in more detail in the next chapter.

2

A personal God: love and faithfulness

————•—••—•————

Every educationalist knows that one of the best teaching aids is a memorable image. Here's a one-liner from the journalist Sydney J. Harris (1917–86) that I came across years ago when trying to work out how best to instil the basics of Christian theology into my students! 'Pupils are more like oysters than sausages.' What exactly did he mean by that? I paused and tried to work it out. Happily, an explanation followed: 'The job of teaching is not to stuff them and then seal them up, but to help them open and reveal the riches within.'[1]

My own experience as an educationalist suggests that this isn't entirely true! But that's not the point. The visual image presents us with a powerful and memorable way of understanding an educational idea. Here's another of Harris's one-liners that I find quite superb: 'The whole purpose of education is to turn mirrors into windows.' Can you see what he's getting at? This time I think he might be right.

As human beings we love images and find them immensely helpful in organizing and developing our ideas – including our ideas of God. In the previous chapter we saw how these images or analogies of God act as 'windows', allowing us to engage God with both our minds and our imaginations. The parables of Jesus of Nazareth draw on the everyday rural life of the area around Galilee to speak to us, so a lost sheep or a growing seed can become a window into the mystery of the kingdom of God.

Yet images also serve another important function: they offer us 'scaled-down' versions to help us grasp things. When finite minds encounter infinite reality, they struggle to express what they encounter. Using analogies is one way of coping with this, allowing our fallen and finite minds to grasp enough of the reality of God to keep us going in our faith. John Calvin is one of many theologians down the ages who has emphasized how God 'adapts to' or 'accommodates' our limited capabilities.

We looked at Plato's famous analogy of the cave in *Faith and the Creeds*. It's time to pay a quick return visit. You will recall that Plato asks us to imagine a group of people who have lived their entire lives trapped within an underground cave. They know nothing of a world beyond – their vision of reality is limited to this dark, shadowy place, illuminated only by firelight.

Try to think yourself into this situation. You may feel deep within that there has to be more to life than this smoky and shadowy realm! But you can't prove it. It's easy to see why Plato's prisoners in the cave would believe that reality is limited to their present surroundings.

Now imagine someone finds her way into the cave from the outside world – from the real world of fresh air, bright sunlight, trees, mountains and brilliant blue skies. How could she explain to you what this other world was like when neither you nor anyone else in the cave knows anything about it? The answer is simple: she would use analogies. She would use things within the world of the cave as signposts to the greater reality that lies beyond it – a reality she knows about and the people inside the cave don't.

She would want to tell you about trees. Noticing a few bits of wood lying around the cave, she would explain that trees were a bit like this but much, much bigger! And they were living! And they were covered with bright green leaves! She would tell you that trees are *like* bits of wood – but they are *more than that*.

Or she might notice a puddle of stagnant water in the corner of the cave. In the outside world, she would say, we have rivers and lakes. A lake is like that puddle – except it's bigger and more beautiful. Once more the same theme would emerge – *it's similar, but so much more*.

When we say that God is our shepherd we're saying that God is like a shepherd – but is so much more than that. It's a great start. The image helps us visualize God's care, guidance and protection – it tells us God journeys with us. We need to build on the foundation of this powerful picture as we lay out the rich biblical witness to God.

Let's take the very familiar biblical image that we touched on in the previous chapter – God as a rock. Now remembering that an analogy is meant to show that two things are similar rather than identical, we must expect to find aspects of the comparison that need to be filtered out. Someone might think that 'God is a rock' means 'God is lifeless', but that would contradict the many images of God that emphasize God's vitality and power. What about our second image: God as a shepherd? This powerfully conveys not that God is a human being but that human shepherds do certain things that can help us understand more about God's dealings with us.

Many of us find we focus on one or two biblical images of God that speak to us deeply and powerfully. There's nothing wrong with that as long as we remember that God cannot be defined exclusively in one image. Indeed, the task of Christian theology is to ensure that many analogies are brought together to give us the fullest possible picture of God. When Paul declares (Ephesians 1.21) that God is 'above every name that is named', he is making two points. First, that God exceeds in greatness any other 'named' person and is not subject to any human authority – past, present or future. And second, that no single named part of the created order is adequate to do justice to who God is and what God is like.

However, let's now explore further the particular way of addressing God that has been honoured and revered within the Christian Church for centuries.

I believe in God the Father

As we saw in the last chapter, the creeds help us put into words our trust in 'the God and Father of our Lord Jesus Christ, the Father of mercies and the God of all consolation' (2 Corinthians 1.3). One reason why the creeds begin by talking about believing in God as 'Father' is because this is the way of speaking *about* God and speaking *to* God used by Jesus of Nazareth. The Gospels emphasize how Jesus of Nazareth spoke of God as his 'Father'. Indeed, the Lord's Prayer – widely regarded as a 'model prayer' for Christians – opens with the phrase 'Our Father'. So in using this language, the creeds are simply following the example of Jesus. Christians believe and trust in the same God who was known, obeyed, and revealed by him.

Let's clear up one common misunderstanding immediately: to speak of God as 'Father' *does not mean that God is male*; nor does it mean we have to invent a female God who is a mother. The Bible and the long history of Christian reflection on this text are quite clear: God *creates* male and female but God *is* neither male nor female. Gender is part of the created order, but the social roles that are sometimes linked with gender throughout human history are not divinely ordained. They are simply cultural contingencies, which change over time.

Why then do so many Christians refer to God as 'he'? The issue here is human language, not the nature of God. In English, as in many other languages, there are three options for referring to living things: 'he', 'she' and 'it'. As we shall see, the Christian understanding of God is strongly personal, and to remain faithful to this essential insight we do need to speak of God as 'he' or 'she' (for it would make no sense to speak of God as 'it'). Many Christians still prefer to use male pronouns – 'he', 'his' and 'him' – to refer to God, for perfectly understandable reasons. Yet God transcends the human distinction between the sexes. God is neither man nor woman but God – and our language struggles to express God's distinct characteristics.

The Bible certainly uses many male role models to speak about God – such as father, king and shepherd – and it is quite easy to overlook the fact that female role models appear, too. The most striking of these are maternal, likening God to a mother giving birth to, or caring for, her young. Clement of Alexandria, a third-century writer who held progressive views on the role of women, tried to provide a comprehensive account of the manner in which God cares for and nourishes us. Augustine of Hippo

(354–430), perhaps the greatest western theologian, also emphasized the maternal aspects of God's love for humanity, along with Jesus of Nazareth's compassion for his followers:

> The one who has promised us heavenly food has nourished us on milk, showing the tenderness of a mother. For just as a mother, suckling her infant, transfers from her flesh the very same food which otherwise would be unsuited to an infant (the little one actually receives what he would have received at table but the food conveyed through the flesh is adapted to the child), so our Lord, in order to convert his wisdom into milk for our benefit, came to us clothed in flesh.[2]

A similar point was made by Anselm of Canterbury in the eleventh century. In one of his more intimate meditations, Anselm reflected on the maternal aspects of the ministry of Jesus of Nazareth:

> And you, Jesus, are you not also a mother?
> Are you not the mother who, like a hen,
> gathers her chickens under her wings?
> Truly, Lord, you are a mother;
> for both they who are in labour
> and they who are brought forth
> are accepted by you.[3]

This rich imagery helps lodge a series of themes in our imagination: that we owe our origins to God; that God brought us into being; that God cares and provides for us. This is a good starting point for reflecting further on one of the most important insights of the creed: that God is not an abstract principle or power but a personal reality. We shall consider this in the next section.

A personal God

All of us like to complain about our employers. I met up with someone I had known back in the days when I was a research student in Oxford. Over a cup of tea I asked him how he was getting on at the college where he now worked. He spent the next 20 minutes relating how awful things were while I sipped my tea, wondering when I might get a word in. He was angry. His employers, he declared, were so obsessed with targets and budgets that they didn't care about the well-being of their employees. 'They behave like machines! They don't care for us as people! They're so *impersonal!*'

Why do people feel so strongly about this? Why is 'impersonal' regarded as such a negative word? My conversation with my friend made clear that he felt his employers were treating him as an object. They were only interested in numbers, statistics and costs; they weren't behaving like real people who cared for others and valued their individuality.

That's a core theme of the Christian understanding of God. We see this concern for the individual in the encounters of Jesus of Nazareth recorded in the Gospels. He treats everyone he meets as if they have their own distinct identity and value. When I first began to read closely through passages describing Jesus' encounter with the woman at the well (John 4) or with Zacchaeus (Luke 19), one of the things that most impressed me was the way he engaged with these people on their own terms. They are not reduced to stereotypes but are treated as being special and significant in their own right. Whatever their faults and failings they are valued for who they are. In his dealings with others, Jesus mirrors a personal God who is concerned with us as individuals.

This is a precious insight. Jesus of Nazareth is not a religious teacher who points us towards the truth, as if that were distinct and separable from who he is. He *is* the truth. He does not simply *show* us the way, he *is* the way (John 14.6). We need to put out of our minds the kind of conceptual God we read about in dull theological textbooks, with their systems of abstractions, focus on propositions and obsession with logic. God is encountered primarily through reading and hearing the greatest story ever told, in the joyful worship of the people of God and through the lives and witness of people who have known and been changed by God. All of these reveal a personal God – one we know (and don't just know about), who encounters and relates to us.

The idea of a personal God is expressed in both the Old and New Testaments in two ways, the first being through the *name* of God. Now imagine you're part of a banking house or firm of lawyers. You're trying to come up with a slogan to draw in customers: is it possible the phrase 'a name you can trust' might be one to reach for? It suggests a hard-earned reputation based on reliability and stability. You would be communicating the message, 'Look at the way we behaved in the past. We're still the same company. You can trust us today!'

For many biblical writers, a name conveyed someone's personal identity and characteristics. Especially in the Old Testament, the character of God is understood to be summarized and expressed in the name of God. Calling 'on the name of the LORD' in times of trouble (Joel 2.32) is about appealing to a known God; it is an expression of love and confidence as much as need and anxiety. The 'LORD God of Israel' is the God who could be trusted in the past – as, for example, in the exodus from Egypt and the entry into the Promised Land. God's name and nature haven't changed. And God can still be trusted today.

The second way the idea of a personal God is expressed is through the image of the 'face of God'. To see the face of God was a mark of favour, intimacy and acceptance. If a ruler wanted to rebuff one of his subjects, he would turn his face away from him. And when the Psalmist felt far from God, he used this same imagery to express his fear of rejection and abandonment. 'O Lord, why do you cast me off? Why do you hide your face from me?' (Psalm 88.14). To see the face of God was to be reassured of both the reality and the favour of God. It is no accident that the New Testament pulsates with excitement over one of its most significant themes – that in Jesus of Nazareth, we can see the glorious face of God (2 Corinthians 4.6).

This strongly personal notion of God is also reflected in the Christian vision of heaven. Some argue that the ultimate goal of humanity is to lose our distinct identity, so that we become like drops of water in an ocean. Christianity takes a very different view. We matter to God as individuals – God knows each of us and values our personal identity. The courts of the New Jerusalem are not occupied by disembodied spirits, purged of their history and memories. We shall be there as ourselves – renewed and healed but recognizably continuous with our earthly selves. The relationship with God that we knew on earth will be continued and consummated in heaven.

In fact the Bible often speaks of God in terms that only really make sense within a personal relationship. God is trustworthy – that is to say, someone who can be relied upon. God is a friend who doesn't let us down, a companion who doesn't abandon us when things go wrong. We can trust God as we might trust caring parents who love us – despite our failings – because they have brought us into this world and want us to enjoy life in all its fullness. God doesn't just speak to us, as if our faith was about being told what to do all the time. God speaks to us to make promises to us – to reassure us that we will not be alone or abandoned. Like a faithful shepherd, God is by our side, helping us to tell right from wrong, encouraging us as we travel and finally bringing us to the New Jerusalem.

The realization that God is a person also helps us make sense of other aspects of our faith, including both the way we think and the way we live. For example, Paul uses the idea of 'reconciliation' – the restoration of a relationship between two persons – as a way of helping us understand the work of Christ (2 Corinthians 5.18–19), something we'll have more to say about in *Lord and Saviour: Jesus of Nazareth*. And it also helps us understand the importance of prayer in the Christian life. Prayer is best seen as a way of deepening our relationship with God, allowing us to share our deepest needs and fears. We spend time with our friends because we love them for their own sake and want to keep our relationship with them active and meaningful. So it is with our relationship with God. We miss the point of prayer if we think of it solely in utilitarian terms – as a kind of 'wants list' that we present to God. Its primary role is to keep close to God, knowing that God will keep close to us.

There's one more point that we need to make here. One of the great fears of our age is depersonalization – being reduced to a statistic, to a number in a database or a social category. We see this at its most brutal in the Nazi extermination camp at Auschwitz, where those selected for slave labour had numbers tattooed on their forearms. Their names were forgotten – they were dehumanized, reduced to a number. Most of us want to protest against this erosion of personal identity – we matter as individuals; we have names not numbers; we are being treated as if we were *objects* when we long to be treated as *persons*! That's one of the reasons why the Christian vision of God as a personal being is so important. *God is the guarantor of our personal identity*. God treats each of us as a person, not an object. God calls and knows each of us by name. The world may treat us as impersonal objects but God is the one who really matters and God knows each of us by name. 'Do not fear, for I have redeemed you; I have called you by name, you are mine' (Isaiah 43.1).

We've now sketched some reasons why Christians speak of a personal God – but more needs to be said on this, so let's dig a little deeper. When I first began to study theology seriously at Oxford back in the 1970s, I came across the writings of the philosopher Martin Buber (1878–1965). One of the central questions Buber explored was what it means to be a 'person'.[4] What, he asked, is the difference in the way we relate to an object – like a pencil – and the way we respond to another human being?

Now the answer may be obvious, but it's still important. I can put together a list of things I know about a pencil – its shape, weight, colour and length. And I can do the same with a human being, noting a friend's build, weight, colouring and height. The lists are similar in many ways, but with the pencil I can *only* know about it – there is just one level of engagement available, whereas with a human being we have access to two levels. I can *know about* someone (what their blood group is, for example) and I can *know* them – that is to say, have some kind of relationship with them, perhaps as a friend or colleague, perhaps as a lover. C. S. Lewis made a famous distinction between 'knowledge-about' and 'knowledge-by-acquaintance'. The former is factual knowledge; the latter is about something much deeper – an encounter, in which we 'taste' the other.[5]

It is possible to get the two rather muddled. The reason so many people read magazines or online articles about celebrities is because we feel we're being allowed privileged access to their real life and secrets. It's like being allowed to peep into something that we're not really meant to know about. Yet we realize that knowing some gossip about some celebrity doesn't mean we've become their best friend. Deep down we're perfectly aware that knowing about the President of the United States is not the same as knowing the President! Relationships are two-way, as we'll discuss further below.

God as a person: four insights

Appreciating that God is personal is central to a right understanding of the creeds. Let's look at four insights that will help us grasp this more fully. First, in speaking of God as a person we're making it clear we can know things about God – for example, that God is gracious, righteous and faithful. We can go further and say that Jesus of Nazareth is the 'image of the invisible God' (Colossians 1.15), *showing* us – not merely *telling us* – what God is like.

But that is rather a detached and disinterested knowledge of God – a knowing of him in the way we might know something about the geography of France without ever caring very much whether we visit it or not. The way the New

Testament speaks of Christian faith has much more to do with a living relationship in which we don't just *know about* God but are granted the privilege of *knowing* God – 'this is eternal life, that they may know you, the only true God, and Jesus Christ whom you have sent' (John 17.3). To 'know' God in this sense is about experiencing, loving and desiring God.

Let's move on to the second point. Suppose you want to begin a friendship with someone but that person isn't drawn to you in the same way. It's tough, but that's just the way things are! Friendship involves delight, and the spark has to be there for both parties before a relationship takes off – it takes two to tango. However, the Christian understanding of God is that of a gracious and loving Lord, who is all too ready to enter into a personal relationship with us. God has taken the initiative in coming to us in Christ, and eagerly awaits our response. God *wants* to relate to us and *invites* us to respond. We're not gatecrashing our way into God's presence – we've been invited. And God has done everything necessary to clear the way for us to come – we just have to say 'yes' to God's invitation.

The third insight is that this way of thinking helps us make sense of growing in our faith. What do we mean when we speak of deepening our faith? When I was starting out as a Christian I thought that this meant acquiring additional factual information about Christianity. I spent lots of time learning the geography of the Holy Land and the dates of various kings of ancient Israel. It didn't seem to help me grow in my faith at all!

Rather, just as we need to spend time with someone and increase the level of our commitment to that person in order for a relationship to flourish, so faith develops when we devote ourselves to worship and prayer and begin to absorb the insights of those who have travelled further on the journey than we have. I found that spiritual writers like Thomas à Kempis helped me go deeper into the gospel and showed me how to develop a richer vision of my faith.

Finally, this way of thinking about God helps us to understand the nature of revelation. What we mean by 'revelation' is not that God merely gives us some information. It's fatally easy to think in terms of God sending us texts – or spiritual prompts – from a safe distance. That's part of the picture but it's *only* part of it. In the deeper and fuller sense of the term, revelation is about God taking the initiative to come in person to *show* us – not merely *tell* us – what God is like.

How do we see God in Jesus Christ? We will have more to say about that in the next volume. We see God mirrored in what Jesus does. Jesus' tears over the death of his friend Lazarus reflect God's compassion at the frailty of our situation (John 11). Jesus giving himself up to death on the cross demonstrates God's love and utter commitment to us.

A God who remembers us

In 2008 I began to research a new biography of C. S. Lewis. This involved reading everything he had written in chronological order, as well as the large amount of literature about him. I came across many early photographs of Lewis and his friends from the 1910s and 1920s. Some showed him with small groups of people; others as part of larger gatherings. It was easy to identify Lewis himself and some of those who played an important role in his life – such as his father, his brother Warren and his childhood friend Arthur Greeves.

Lewis would correspond with Arthur for over half a century, right up to his death in 1963.

But there were people neither I nor any of those I consulted – who had expert knowledge of Lewis's family history – could identify. All too often I had to pencil the word 'unknown' beside their images, though it was obvious they were important members of Lewis's circle of friends. Once they mattered; now they were forgotten – the memories of them and their identities had simply faded out of history like the ink on a piece of writing paper washed away by a spilt glass of water. 'For there is no enduring remembrance of the wise or of fools, seeing that in the days to come all will have been long forgotten' (Ecclesiastes 2.16).

People like to be remembered. We want to feel it made a difference to someone that we were here; that we helped others at critical moments; that our living mattered in however small a way. Most of us, however, do not leave much of a legacy. The only thing that can stop us disappearing into the mists of the past is a deliberate decision by those who come after us to honour our memory.

In England the devastating impact of the First World War (1914–18) is recalled every November in services of remembrance in which the names of those who fell in battle are read, 'lest we forget'. In the Cotswold village of Alvescot, in which I have the privilege of ministering, the names of the dead were written out by hand many years ago in black ink, carefully and lovingly, so that those visiting the church would remember them. The list is still there *but the ink is fading*. The day will eventually come when the names will no longer be visible.

The great fear of Old Testament writers was that they would be forgotten by others, and even by God. When the people of Jerusalem were in exile in the great city of Babylon, they wondered if God had remembered them. After all, they were far from their homeland. Maybe some of them thought of the Lord as a local deity who was unconcerned with what was happening outside the land of Israel. That would explain the enormous force of sections of the prophecy of Isaiah that speak of God remembering his exiled people. 'Remember these things, O Jacob, and Israel, for you are my servant; I formed you, you are my servant; O Israel, you will not be forgotten by me' (Isaiah 44.21).

This important theme of being remembered is brought home in the powerful image of the intimate relationship between a mother and her infant child.

> Zion said, 'The LORD has forsaken me,
>> my Lord has forgotten me.'
> Can a woman forget her nursing-child,
>> or show no compassion for the child of her womb?
> Even these may forget,
>> yet I will not forget you.
> See, I have inscribed you on the palms of my hands.
>> (Isaiah 49.14–16)

Here the rich analogy of God as a mother who would never forget her child is supplemented with a dramatic turn of phrase: the names of the people of God are 'inscribed' on God's hands. They are permanently etched into God's very being; God remembers us even when we fail to remember God.

So why might we forget God? One obvious answer is time pressure. A highly stressed job, tight deadlines and anxiety all crowd in, squeezing thoughts of God from our minds. One of the most famous prayers on this theme was written by Jacob Astley (1579–1652), a royalist commander, as he prepared for the Battle of Edgehill (1642) during the English Civil War (1642–51): 'O Lord, Thou knowest how busy I must be this day; if I forget Thee, do not Thou forget me.' We all need to find quiet times when we can recall and reconnect with God.

Sometimes the reason we forget God is because we're compelled to. The brutal enforcement of atheism during the period of the Soviet Union (1922–91) led to the attempted erasure of memories of God. The Czech novelist Milan Kundera (b.1929) saw how power groups tried to get people to forget things that stood in their way. 'The struggle of humanity against power is the struggle of memory against forgetting.' Churches need to develop strategies to ensure that the cultural memory of God is sustained when they are confronted by people or groups who wish to eradicate it for their own ends – which they present, of course, as being for the good of society as a whole.

Forgetting God can happen in other circumstances. The fact that people are living longer means more are experiencing memory loss in old age. Memory loss can lead to individuals losing much of their identity and eventually being unable even to recognize spouses, children or lifelong friends. God, too, is forgotten.[6] It is very difficult for the person's dear ones, who feel a sense of bereavement as the person they once knew seems to vanish.

In these situations, we need to try and see beyond the tragic changes in our loved ones and to hold fast to the truth that God does not forget us, even though we may forget God. If our failing memory means we are no longer capable of remembering those we once loved, let us trust that God remembers us. Old age has never been easy. We may recall the Psalmist asking God to be with him in the declining years when things began to fall apart. 'Do not cast me off in the time of old age; do not forsake me when my strength is spent' (Psalm 71.9). We are held in the memories of God, who will remember us properly no matter what happens to us on earth. God will uphold a relationship with us, though we get to the point when we can no longer sustain it from our side. At that stage we simply have to entrust ourselves to God – we may feel like the lost sheep that was so tired it couldn't make its own way back to the safety of the sheepfold, but God, the good shepherd, will find us and carry us home (Luke 15.4–7).

That's all part of what it means to speak of God as 'Father'.

3

An almighty God: power, compassion and suffering

It is among my most vivid memories of my early schooldays. One lunchtime, when I was about seven years old, I got into a heated conversation with two classmates over whose father was the most important. Every school playground in the world has probably witnessed conversations just like this.

'My father's a butcher! And that means he makes lots of money!' We digested this piece of information. Not to be outdone, I joined in. 'My father's a doctor! That means he can heal people! You need people like that if you get sick!' This, however, paled into insignificance compared with what the third member of our little group had to say. 'Well, my dad's a policeman. That means he can throw you into jail! He can do anything he likes!' At that time none of us had any real understanding of such things as legal frameworks and citizens' rights, so we had no doubt about whose father really mattered.

It was an unsettling thought for my seven-year-old mind – the idea of going to jail didn't sound like much fun, so my friends and I decided we'd better stay on the right side of the policeman's son. He was very open to this idea and help-fully suggested that we could make sure of his favour and our own safety by helping him out in a few ways – such as doing his homework.

At that age I tended to think of God as a cosmic police-man. He could do anything he liked, and as there was nobody more important, no one could argue with him. I didn't really like the sound of this God very much. He seemed like someone who made the rules up as he went along and turned mere whims into commandments.

But that's the way lots of people think of 'the almighty' we speak of in the creeds. Even Christians sometimes imagine God as a Tudor monarch with limitless power. And they regard prayer as a means of making sure you're on the right side of God – a bit like the Tudor court factions who threw morality to the winds in trying to win the favour of the monarch to advance their own interests. In a world in which power and influence matter, it's natural to assume the almighty will outrank and outperform everyone else.

The Nazi dictator Adolf Hitler had no hesitation in referring to God as 'the almighty'.[1] For Hitler, God was supreme power – someone you want on your side. But as the Swiss theologian Karl Barth pointed out in a series of lectures given just after the Second World War, to define God in terms of power is ultimately to deify power. And absolute power has the potential to be diabolical – something destructive and evil that appeals to those who want to advance their own ends.[2] We need to think carefully about what it means to speak of God as 'almighty', and avoid falling into misleading ways of thinking.

Can an almighty God do everything?

It's easy to see why so many people think that believing in an 'almighty' God means believing in a God who can do anything and everything – after all, God is God. But when you begin to think about this, you realize it's not that simple. Let's consider a few questions and see where they take us.

Can God draw a triangle with four sides? The answer is clearly not. Triangles have three sides; to draw a shape with four sides is to draw something else – four-sided triangles do not and cannot exist. The fact that God cannot draw a triangle with four sides is not a problem; it just forces us to restate our simple statement in a more complicated way. 'To say that God is almighty means that God can do anything that does not involve logical contradiction.'

Now this is a good start, but it soon becomes clear that there are difficulties even with this modified definition. Let's ask another question to help us identify the problem: can God break promises?

There is no logical contradiction involved in breaking promises. Nor is it something that's difficult to do. Sadly, most of us have broken a promise at some point in our lives, even if it was with the greatest reluctance. So if God can do anything that does not involve logical contradiction, God can certainly break a promise.

The reasoning seems impeccable, yet many readers will be uneasy with this line of thought – the idea of God breaking promises doesn't seem right; it seems to reduce God to our level; it suggests God is like fallen and fallible human beings! Let's ask another question: can God tell lies? Once more, it's not something that's difficult to do. Many in this cynical world of ours would argue that some people rely on lying to keep themselves in business. And if human beings can deliberately deceive people, surely God can too? After all, there's no *logical* problem here, so we might conclude that an all-powerful God can lie – even better than we can.

Except we know that our God just doesn't break promises. Christianity is about a trustworthy God, and that there is no way this God could or would lie. Maybe no logical principles would be infringed if God behaved in such a way, but something much deeper would be violated – our understanding of the character of God. Logic lets us down here. There's something deeper at stake – God's character.

There is a world of difference between a whimsical god – like some of Homer's unpleasantly self-centered Olympian deities, who constantly needed to be cajoled and humoured – and a faithful God who may be relied upon and trusted. The creeds make it clear which God they are talking about – and it's not one of Homer's.

For Christians, God is trustworthy and faithful – and trustworthy and faithful people just don't do these kinds of things. They stand by what they promise. Everything in the biblical witness to the nature and character of God protests against a God who would deceive or lie. 'The LORD your God is a merciful God, he will neither abandon you nor destroy you; he will not forget the covenant with your ancestors that he swore to them' (Deuteronomy 4.31). Indeed, the Hebrew word most biblical translations render as 'truth' really means 'something that you can rely on'. God makes promises – and having made those promises, stands by them. God tells us the truth about the way things are, even if we may find this hard to bear at times. The faith of both Israel and the Christian Church is grounded on the faithfulness of a God who makes promises and remains true to them.

In 1801, the London Stock Exchange was founded, replacing the coffee houses of seventeenth-century London as the hub of British financial life. Stocks and shares were sold without any written pledges or documentation. The traders were all gentlemen and knew and trusted each other absolutely. The motto the Stock Exchange adopted reflected this: *dictum meum pactum* – 'my word is my bond'.

The world's banking system still depends on precisely this same trust, and breaking it has serious consequences – as was seen during the financial crisis of 2008 when markets across the globe teetered on the brink of disaster. Yes, you *can* break promises, even when others trust and rely on you, but no one would regard such behaviour as a virtuous expression of freedom and integrity. It simply makes you seem untrustworthy and unreliable.

The gospel is about a God who may be trusted; whose promises may be relied upon. We all need a secure base for our lives, and for Christians the anchor is a faithful God who is always there for us. God's faithfulness is a character trait – it expresses the way God is.

So our investigation of God as 'almighty' has led to the conclusion that this does not mean God *can* do or *chooses* to do *anything*, nor that God ceases to be righteous or merciful; rather it means that God acts powerfully – yet also righteously and mercifully. God wills what is right for us, and is able to achieve it. God does not just *promise* us salvation; God has the ability to achieve our salvation. 'The one who calls you is faithful, and he will do this (1 Thessalonians 5.24).

An almighty God: power and character

In 1887, the British politician and historian Lord Acton (1834–1902) observed that 'power tends to corrupt, and absolute power corrupts absolutely'. As a result, 'great men are almost always bad men'. It is an idea that has shaped our assumptions about public office and the risks of concentrating too much power in too few hands. Human nature is morally fragile and is placed under such severe stress by the temptations and privileges of power that it often proves incapable of resisting them.

This theme lies at the heart of one of the greatest works of twentieth-century literature – J. R. R. Tolkien's *The Lord of the Rings*. The master ring seemed to offer power to its possessors – but in reality it enslaved them. Tolkien shrewdly realized that the possibility of possessing absolute power revealed what people were really like. Power acts like a mirror of the soul: when we can do what we like, we show people what we would like to do. The American President Abraham Lincoln (1809–65) put this point well when he said, 'If you want to test a man's character, give him power.'

Nowhere is this more thrillingly illustrated than in the Gospel temptation narratives. Before Jesus of Nazareth began his public ministry in Galilee he was tempted in the wilderness – these temptations were all about the abuse of power (Matthew 4.1–11). Why not turn stones into bread? What a magnificent act of theatre! Why not throw yourself off the roof of the temple so that squadrons of angels come to your rescue? That would be really impressive! But Jesus' ministry is to be about using power to help others, never himself, and he turns the tempter down. It's an issue of identity, integrity and character.

The Old Testament writers understood this point completely. God, they declared, was 'merciful and gracious, slow to anger, and abounding in steadfast love and faithfulness, keeping steadfast love for the thousandth generation' (Exodus 34.6–7). Israel did not know or believe in a whimsical God whose faithfulness might vanish overnight. Rather, Israel's God was one whose behaviour reflected God's identity and character – God could be trusted.

Yet many would rightly want to raise a question at this point. If God is indeed in charge of things, why do they often seem to go so badly wrong? Why is there pain and suffering in the world? Why is there so much injustice and evil?

God and the darkness of faith

When I was young my family took vacations in County Donegal in the north-west of Ireland. We loved its beautiful beaches and rugged countryside. However, Atlantic rainstorms, sweeping in from the west, made Donegal a very wet place indeed, and one of my main memories of those distant days is sitting inside the family car, waiting for the rain to stop. On these occasions my parents would open a Thermos flask of coffee. The steam condensed on the cold windows and every now and then my father would get out his handkerchief to wipe the glass and check if it was still raining. Donegal was still there, of course; it was just that we couldn't see it very well through our misted windows – it was blurred and fuzzy.

There are times when we feel that way about our experience of life – some things are just bewildering. Where is God in suffering and pain? Why does God allow catastrophic events to happen? These questions, which have been asked by Christians down the ages, bring us to the heart of the idea of 'providence' – that 'all things work together for good for those who love God' (Romans 8.28). I think we will need to be realistic about how far we can go towards understanding this concept.

A major change in western culture began to take place in the eighteenth century, as the 'Age of Reason' dawned in Europe and America. One of the results of this movement – sometimes referred to as the Enlightenment – was an increased emphasis on clear, logical answers. Fuzziness and imprecision were seen as signs of error, and some theologians and preachers began to change the way they talked about difficult areas of theology – such as the doctrine of providence. Previously, being conscious of the limits of human thought, they had tended to speak cautiously about things that were difficult to understand or put into words, but now slick and easy answers, based on a rigid logic, were offered to deep questions that simply couldn't be answered in those terms. In the end all this did was encourage superficial forms of faith that were incapable of taking on board the complexity of experience and the ambiguities of life.

The hard truth is that some questions just can't be fully answered. In *Faith and the Creeds* we talked about seeing the 'big picture' of the Christian faith that holds everything together. Like a lens, Christianity brings things into sharper focus; like a light, it illuminates a landscape so we can see many details more clearly. But there will always be shadowlands on the landscape, for although God can see the big picture properly, we cannot. As Paul put it, 'we know only in part'; however, 'when the complete comes, the partial will come to an end' (1 Corinthians 13.9–10).

We have to learn to live with our limits. Slick answers are for people who haven't quite grasped what the issues are and are happy to content themselves with shallow and simplistic responses to the deepest riddles of life. Christianity recognizes that we are restricted in terms of our reason and our grasp of reality – since we can't see properly, things are always going to seem fuzzy and blurred.

It is helpful here to turn to the book of Job, one of the finest pieces of reflection on the place of suffering in the world. When I was younger I hoped that the story of Job would give me some quick and easy answers to my questions about why God allowed suffering. I didn't find them. Initially I was discouraged and somewhat irritated by this, but as I've grown older and kept on reading the text, I've become much more appreciative of its wisdom. Why? Because I find two themes there that seem to me to help put suffering in its proper perspective. The first concerns the neat little theories of suffering offered by Job's well-meaning 'comforters'. All are shown to be inadequate, and the point being made here is that no theory can answer the mystery of suffering. Human language is simply not up to communicating divine realities. Job is forced to confront this.

The second and more important theme is that, in responding to Job's challenge for an answer, God invites him to look at things in a very different way. God allows him to view the big picture, something that transcends anything Job is able to see from his own limited perspective. It is as if a curtain is drawn aside and the vast panorama of the world is revealed. Earlier Job had questioned God, calling into question God's wisdom in allowing his suffering. Now, by gaining a sense of the big picture (impossible for human beings to grasp fully or properly), Job is able to appreciate his own limited and somewhat self-centred view of things.

He realizes he is not in a position to understand fully; that God's wisdom is deeper than his own; and, finally, that he can cope with suffering simply because he knows God really is there.

We need to be aware of what our limits are and avoid unrealistic expectations about what we can know with certainty and see with total clarity. We think we ought to be able to *prove* that certain things are true – that God exists, for example – but that's just not the way things work. Being prepared to accept our limitations is an essential part of growing in faith.

And it's not just people of faith who need to realize the limits of reason! After giving a talk in London a few years ago, I got into discussion with a student who had just started studying philosophy. In a year or two, he told me, he would have sorted out all the big questions of life using nothing more than human reason – he would only believe what reason could prove. Everything was so simple! I asked him to prove to me that reason was completely reliable – after all, I pointed out, we needed to check it out before we trusted it! The young man had clearly given this question no thought, and after a few inconclusive stabs at answers he walked away, frustrated and angry.

Paradoxically, it's only when we use our reason to the full that we begin to appreciate its limits. The French philosopher Blaise Pascal put this rather well: 'Reason's final step is to realize that there are an infinite number of things that lie beyond it. It is simply feeble if it does not get as far as realizing that.'[3] This doesn't mean we can't reflect on issues such as the character of God – it just means we need to be suspicious of the slick and easy answers some offer us.

So are we dealing with a God who tricks us, who abandons us, is unjust and unreliable? We see this question being explored in a famous dialogue between Abraham and God early in the book of Genesis. Abraham is puzzled by what is happening around him, wondering how God fits into things, how a righteous God would act. In the end he comes to his conclusion: 'Shall not the Judge of all the earth do what is just?' (Genesis 18.25). It is both a question and a statement – Abraham realizes he has no option other than to trust God. He doesn't see the full picture but he knows and trusts a God who he believes to be worthy of that trust.

This is a position we all find ourselves in from time to time – we don't see the big picture. We have to make decisions about what is really going on and whom we can really trust. Who will stay with us when things get tough and won't let us down if things go wrong? It's a theme we find throughout western literature – the need to trust someone as our guide and mentor.

While I was a student I went to hear a lecture by an army officer who had served in North Africa during the Second World War. He was in charge of a column of trucks that had to be driven through the desert to bring supplies to the front line. Everyone knew there were minefields out there but nobody was quite sure where – except for a local tribesman who had seen the minefields being laid.

We listened as the officer described his predicament. They needed to travel quickly but they had no idea which tracks through the desert were safe and which not. In the end he made a momentous decision: he asked the tribesman to guide them. They set off at high speed, following their guide's directions, having no idea where they were being taken but trusting that he knew what he was doing – and that he was on their side. Many hours later they arrived safely at the front line.

We've all been in that kind of situation – having to trust someone to guide us or help us make big decisions. The biggest decisions in life are often about whom to trust. Being trustworthy is a character trait – if people prove worthy of small confidences, we learn to trust them with more important things.

That's the situation reflected in Abraham's dialogue with God. In the end he decides that what he knows about God is enough to forge a relationship of trust. God does some things for reasons Abraham personally does not understand but he's prepared to believe that these somehow express God's very nature. As the Psalmist later put it, God's actions bring and hold together love, justice and mercy – 'Steadfast love and faithfulness will meet; righteousness and peace will kiss each other' (Psalm 85.10).

So where might we expect to find the guiding hand of God at work? Two main answers have been given: first, in history at large; second, in our own personal lives. Edmund Gibbon (1737–84), in his famous *History of the Decline and Fall of the Roman Empire*, declared that history was 'little more than the register of the crimes, follies, and misfortunes of mankind'. Believing there was no God, Gibbon took the view that the mess of history reflected the moral failures of humanity.

Early Christian writers, however, saw the rapid progress of Christianity in the Roman Empire as a sign of God's providence. Having begun as a despised movement on the fringes of imperial Roman culture, those belonging to the faith gradually grew in numbers and influence. Christianity overcame persecution and official hostility and in the late fourth century became the official religion of the Roman Empire. What better proof could you hope to find of God directing history?! Except that things no longer seemed quite so straightforward a little later on when the western Roman Empire started to collapse after invasion from the north.

Augustine of Hippo began to raise awkward questions about what he perceived as a rather simplistic approach to divine providence. How could history be regarded simply as the outworking of God's providence when frail and fallen human beings were involved? As the Church had grown powerful it had also been tainted by corruption, losing something of its spiritual vitality. Becoming the official religion of the Roman Empire made Christianity the faith of the establishment, leading to the dilution or loss of some of its most important insights. Indeed, many recent Christian theologians now regard the 'Christianization' of the Roman Empire as a backwards step. It may have enhanced the social prestige and political power of Christianity at the time but in other ways it compromised its credentials – most significantly, as a critic of the excesses of Roman political power.

This is not to suggest that God doesn't work in human history; it's really a word of caution against simplistic readings of history of which we human being are, of course, a part. We often mess things up and may feel we're getting in God's way rather than helping things along, though fortunately God can use failure to work out his purposes, just as much as success!

Many of us will find it easier to understand providence in terms of our own personal history. We sense that God's hand is guiding us and that our story matters. Yet it is impossible to read the Bible – or indeed to live from day to day – without sensing that there is a bigger story of which we are part. We may not fully see this; we may find the picture blurry at points and difficult to grasp. But one of the deepest intuitions of the Christian faith, grounded in both Scripture and the long tradition of Christian reflection and experience, is that the threads of our own lives are being woven into something greater and deeper.

We are called into God's story. This means we're not just people who look at this story from outside – we realize we've been invited to be part of it. We've been written into the story and have roles to play and things to do. One way of thinking about faith is to see it as a willingness to become part of God's story – our own story is given significance, meaning and purpose because it becomes part of this greater story.

So how do we help things along, play our roles in this great story? Obviously, just hoping God will sort everything out won't suffice. As responsible Christians we cannot evade our responsibility to pray for wisdom and to try to act wisely. Those drawn to work in the medical fields, relief work or social care often find they have been inspired by a vision of a fallen and frail world that is loved by God. They long to make a difference and, by being part of God's work of transformation and renewal, contribute to the world becoming more like what we know God wants it to be.

God and suffering

For many people the biggest question concerns the existence of suffering and pain in the world. Our deepest intuitions

tell us that things are not meant to be like this; that
something's wrong. But why should we think so? Not
everyone does: Richard Dawkins insists that suffering is
as inevitable as it is meaningless and we simply need
to get used to this. It's a slick answer but it leaves many
unsatisfied. Deep down we know things are not that
straightforward.

G. K. Chesterton argued that from a Christian perspective
joy is the central feature of life, and sorrow is peripheral.
It's a helpful point. Life is complex – we experience times
of sorrow, times of joy; the world around us is beautiful
in places, ugly in others. 'Everything human must have in
it both joy and sorrow; the only matter of interest is the
manner in which the two things are balanced or divided.'[4]
How can we make sense of such a complex, varied reality
that is neither one thing nor another?

Chesterton's answer is important. The world is not a meaningless jumble in which joy and sorrow are randomly thrown
together. The dominant theme is that life is meaningful and
joyful, though tinged with sadness and sorrow. 'Melancholy
should be an innocent interlude, a tender and fugitive frame
of mind; praise should be the permanent pulsation of the
soul.'[5] For as Chesterton realized, this complex world is passing away, to give way to a world in which sadness and sorrow,
pain and tears are no more. We can anticipate what is to
come in the here and now.

Chesterton was clear that the Christian big picture
offers answers to the fundamental questions of life while
leaving some minor issues unresolved. Given the limitations
of the human mind we cannot hope for any worldview
to make total sense of things. For the atheist, Chesterton
suggested, sorrow becomes central and joy peripheral

because atheism can only engage the peripheral questions of life, leaving the central ones unanswered. For Chesterton it's a question of the perspective from which we see suffering. If there is no God then life is dark and gloomy, with occasional flashes of light. But if there is a God, life is bright and good, though shadows and shades remain for the present.

Some argue that the Christian big picture makes suffering into a problem. The real truth is much more interesting – that big picture *allows us to understand why we find suffering to be a problem in the first place*. Let's explore this important point further.

Where do we get our deep intuition that the way things are isn't the way they are meant to be? After all, that is the fundamental concern that leads us to talk about the 'problem of suffering'. For Christians this sense comes from the biblical vision of a good creation that has gone wrong and that will be restored. Christianity's big picture allows us to understand the present order in a particular way – namely, as damaged and broken and in need of mending and restoration.

C. S. Lewis remarked that when he himself was an atheist it seemed obvious that there couldn't be a God – pain and suffering showed that either God did not exist or that God was pointless. Yet as he reflected on this position he began to realize that it did not really make all that much sense.

> My argument against God was that the universe seemed so cruel and unjust. But how had I got this idea of *just* and *unjust*? A man does not call a line crooked unless he has some idea of a straight line. What was I comparing the universe with when I called it unjust?[6]

Lewis's point was simple and cannot be overlooked. Anyone who judges this world to be flawed or 'unjust' bases that judgement on an understanding of what the world *ought* to be like. But where does that norm come from?

For Lewis, Christianity provided the vision of justice and joy that enabled him to view this world as penultimate and provisional. It made sense – to the extent that this was possible – of our own world and experience, while at the same time proclaiming that something better lay ahead, something to be embraced and welcomed when the time came to enter it.

If we look through a Christian lens we see this world of sorrow, pain and suffering set against the great vision of the New Jerusalem in which 'mourning and crying and pain will be no more' (Revelation 21.4). This world seems flawed because we judge it against a higher standard – not a norm we have invented or imagined but one that's an integral part of the Christian big picture. The good always seems inadequate when seen in the light of the best. If there were no New Jerusalem this world would be unsurpassed. Because of the great Christian vision of a renewed creation, a transformed humanity and a place of dwelling in which we shall no longer experience suffering or death, we see our present world in the light of this future hope, and as a result judge it to be deficient or problematic.

At an early stage in my career I was invited to consider a senior position at the University of Geneva in Switzerland. Some of my publications had been very well received there and there was the possibility of a permanent transfer. So I went over from Oxford University to discuss this. It seemed a wonderful prospect: I would have a huge salary, excellent working conditions and the right to live in Switzerland. The university itself was located at the crossroads of Europe, on the shores of beautiful Lake Geneva. What more could I hope for? My Oxford position seemed rather unattractive in comparison! I became restless as the negotiations proceeded, imagining I was already living abroad.

Then a problem developed over how the job description was to be interpreted. We couldn't reach agreement over one critical issue, so I ended up staying in Oxford. Now that Geneva was no longer a possibility, my Oxford job seemed perfectly fine, but that was because I was no longer measuring it against something more attractive!

The point here is simple: every evaluation involves a comparison – real or imagined. The atheist who argues that this is a lousy universe, created by an incompetent or uncaring God, is in a difficult position: nobody can point to another real and known universe against which we can evaluate the one we inhabit. The atheist can only assert his or her *belief* that a better universe is possible but it's nothing more than a belief – an assertion, lacking any evidenced foundation.

God and suffering: understanding and coping

Two great questions arise whenever someone is confronted with suffering, whether in their own lives or the lives of those who matter to them. How can I make sense of this? And how can I cope with this? They are both vital questions – but they are rather different.

C. S. Lewis is one of the most important witnesses to the distinctions between these two approaches to suffering. In 1940 he published a short book entitled *The Problem of Pain*. It was his first work of popular Christian apologetics and was well received. Many continue to find its logical analysis of the 'problem of pain' helpful, even compelling, though the approach Lewis tends to take is to treat the existence of pain and suffering as riddles to be solved; they cause difficulty because they don't seem to fit easily into the big picture of the Christian faith. He famously argues that pain is a wake-up call, demanding that we recognize our own transiency and mortality. 'God whispers to us in our pleasures, speaks in our conscience, but shouts in our pains'; suffering is God's 'megaphone to rouse a deaf world'.[7] Pain thus helps to shatter the illusion that 'all is well', allowing God to plant 'the flag of truth within the fortress of a rebel soul'.

Now there are some excellent points made in this important book, which continues to reward its readers with helpful insights. Yet Lewis seems to regard the experience of suffering itself as unimportant. 'The only purpose of the book,' he explains, 'is to solve the intellectual problem raised by suffering.'[8] Any real-life experience of pain was 'unconnected and irrelevant' to his reflections on its importance.[9] Some readers were left wondering what would happen if Lewis had to endure suffering so great that he could not help but realize the 'problem of pain' was much more than an intellectual issue.

When Lewis was in his late fifties he married Joy Davidman. Tragically, in 1960, only four years later, she died of cancer, and the trauma Lewis experienced forced him to rethink everything. He was overwhelmed with grief. The neat theological slogans of *The Problem of Pain*, such as describing suffering as 'God's megaphone', seemed more than a little trite in the face of the harsh, irreducible realities thrown up by the suffering and death of his wife. Wrestling with a firestorm of emotions and anger, Lewis wrote a blistering account of his spiritual and intellectual turmoil in *A Grief Observed*. Many now regard it as one of the finest accounts of the grieving process, putting into words the seeming hopelessness and helplessness of a bereaved person.

Yet Lewis's searing analysis of his experience reaches a turning point when he begins to reflect more fully on his desire to be able to suffer instead of his wife. 'If only I could bear it, or the worst of it, of any of it, instead of her.'[10] For Lewis this was the mark of a true lover: someone who was willing to take on suffering in order that the beloved might be spared its pain. And at this point Lewis makes the connection that is essential to any Christian attempt to grasp and cope with the reality of suffering – namely, that God chose to suffer for us in Christ. The ultimate answer to suffering is not ultimately an *idea* or a *theory* – though these come into it – but a *person*. In choosing to come into our world, God also chose to enter into our suffering and bear it.

It is not surprising, then, that many Christians, when reflecting on how to grasp and endure suffering, turn to an image rather than a theological textbook. And that image is, of course, the crucified Christ, the 'image of the invisible God' (Colossians 1.15) who enables us to make the crucial connection between a loving and caring God and the realities of human existence. The cross affirms that God has come into the midst of our world in order to bear our suffering, to triumph over it and ultimately deliver us from it. He has willingly shared our pain and grief because we matter to him.

Earlier we noted how the Bible uses both paternal and maternal images to help us grasp something of the nature of God. We are invited to trust God as we would trust a loving parent who is always there for us, even when we travel far from home. We are asked to believe that God's commitment to us is inexhaustible, that God loves us even when we can see few reasons at all for such a generous commitment.

Our thoughts now turn to the next great affirmation of the creeds – that God is the creator of heaven and earth. What is meant by that, and what difference does it make?

4

Creator of heaven and earth

One of my favourite stories from the classical age concerns the Greek philosopher Aristippus (*c.* 435–*c.* 356 BC), who found himself shipwrecked on the Aegean island of Rhodes. He had no idea where he was. Was this strange place uninhabited? Would he be able to find anyone to help him? As he walked along the shoreline he spotted some patterns traced in the sand. Like Robinson Crusoe discovering a footprint on the beach of his deserted island, Aristippus had noticed something that changed his perception of his surroundings and allowed him to regard them in a new way. He realized he was not on his own – there was someone else on the island.

Since the beginning of recorded history, people have looked at the world around us and wondered about its deeper meaning. We see rivers and pastures, stunning mountain ranges in the distance and starry skies above. What are they all about? Where did they come from? Do they point to a bigger story? Is this our true homeland or do we really belong somewhere else? Are there tracings in the fabric of the world that tell us we are not alone? Many answers have been given and debated endlessly.

One of the deepest human intuitions is that this world is not really our home. We are sojourners, passing through on our way to somewhere else. Christianity bases this intuition on its understanding of God and expresses it especially in its understanding of creation.

Introducing the Christian idea of creation

From the outset, Christianity proclaimed that the world around us was not itself divine but was, nevertheless, of divine origin. God brought the universe into existence and in so doing established an order that reflected God's character. Some peoples in the Ancient Near East believed in national gods, whose sphere of influence was limited to a geographical region – such as Egypt or Babylon. For ancient Israel, recognizing God as creator meant that the 'LORD GOD of hosts' was the lord of *all* the world. 'I am the LORD, who made all things, who alone stretched out the heavens, who by myself spread out the earth' (Isaiah 44.24). This idea seems to have become especially important during the period of exile in Babylon, when the people of Israel were far from their own land. They did not need to live in Israel to know, trust and be guided by the God of Israel.

So what is the Christian doctrine of creation? What are its core themes? I believe there are three. In the first place the Christian understanding of creation is about *origination*: the world has not always existed; it came into being – not by accident but by an act of will. To speak of creation is to speak of both the universe and ourselves, its inhabitants, being brought into being by God.

This leads into the second core theme – that of *intentionality*. In plain English, the universe did not come into being as an accident but as the result of a deliberate act. The universe did not simply happen; it was *made* to happen, and it was *meant* to happen.

The third aspect of the language of creation is that of *signification*. The universe is a like a signpost to its creator, pointing beyond itself to its ultimate source and origin. It echoes or expresses the character of God in a scaled-down yet recognizable manner. As G. K. Chesterton put it, 'God was a creator, as an artist is a creator.'[1] The universe bears the imprint of God, revealing something of the divine splendour and wisdom – 'The heavens are telling the glory of God; and the firmament proclaims his handiwork' (Psalm 19.1).

Each of these aspects of the doctrine of creation merits further exploration, beginning with the theme of origination. The Christian view that the universe came into being was widely criticized during the period of the early Church by secular writers, most of whom believed that the world had existed eternally. Christians found themselves facing ridicule. How could anyone in the sophisticated Greek cultural world take the Christian faith seriously when it contradicted one of the core teachings of the great philosopher Aristotle?

Similar ideas were deeply embedded in the scientific community in the not so distant past. By the first decade of the twentieth century, most scientists had come to the view that the universe had always existed. Any talk of 'creation' was meaningless, and thinking of the universe as having an 'origin' was outdated religious nonsense that science had rightly consigned to the intellectual rubbish bin. Maybe the universe had altered over time, but the scientific wisdom of that age was that it was absurd to suggest that it had a beginning – or that it would have an end.

How things have changed![2] From around 1920, growing evidence began to suggest that the world originated in what we now call the big bang (a cosmic fireball that expanded to form our present universe), though the scientific community decisively accepted this new way of thinking only after the Second World War. One of the reasons for their reluctance was the belief that this seemed a very 'religious' way of thinking! Atheist astronomers such as Fred Hoyle (1915–2001) were alarmed that this new scientific understanding of the origins of the universe seemed uncomfortably close to a Christian viewpoint. In the end, however, such atheistic prejudice was overcome – the idea that the universe came into being is now mainstream science.

However, agreement that the universe had an origin does not necessarily mean there is a God or that the Christian doctrine of creation is right. It certainly *suggests* these things; it is *consistent* with them; but it does not *prove* them. Some atheist scientists would argue that the universe just happened. Maybe it came into being by a process we don't understand; maybe it even caused its own creation. Not unreasonably, Christians point out that these seem rather clumsy ways of trying to avoid the obvious fact that what we now know about the origins of the universe fits neatly into the Christian 'big picture' way of thinking.

The second aspect of the doctrine of creation, intentionality, affirms that God meant to create the world – and us. This world is not an accident and nor are we. We can speak of life having a purpose and the universe having a meaning. However, these are not ideas to be read off the world, like colour, temperature or height: they are more profound notions, lying beneath the surface of things. The book of Job, which we discussed a little while ago, speaks of wisdom as something that is hidden deep within the world, its true meaning concealed from a casual and superficial glance. Meaning and purpose are things we need to discover, if we are able, and to be told about, if we are not.

The doctrine of creation gives us a lens for looking at the worlds around and within us. When I was young I often lay awake at night tracing the patterns of the stars through my school dormitory window. I found this a deeply melancholy experience as I had rejected any belief in God, and believed I was alone in a vast, meaningless universe. Those silent pinpoints of light in the night sky became symbols of the brevity of my own existence and the futility of life.

After discovering Christianity I looked again at those same stars but now through a different lens. What I had once seen as symbols of transience and pointlessness took on a new meaning – the God who had created those had also created me. Even though I was insignificant in relation to the grand scale of the cosmos, I was known, loved and valued by God.

> When I look at your heavens, the work of your fingers,
>   the moon and the stars that you have established;
> what are human beings that you are mindful of them,
>   mortals that you care for them?
> Yet you have made them a little lower than God,
>   and crowned them with glory and honour.
>
> (Psalm 8.3–5)

Our third aspect of the doctrine of creation – signification – insists that God's character, like that of any artist, is expressed in God's creation. When understood correctly, the world around us echoes and reflects something of God. The truth is that nature on its own is very ambiguous. We may take delight in beautiful sunsets and rich landscapes but what about the bloodshed of the food chain? What of the pain animals inflict on each other in their quest for fresh meat? We need a map to make sense of the complex moral landscape of nature, and a lens to help us bring things into focus. We need to know how to interpret something that is ambivalent, so that we can see it in the right way; otherwise the moral ambiguity of nature might lead us to think that God is both good and evil – or perhaps that there are two Gods, one good and one evil.

G. K. Chesterton expressed the importance of interpretation forcefully: 'A man loves Nature in the morning for her innocence and amiability, and at nightfall, if he is loving her still, it is for her darkness and her cruelty.'[3] The natural world needs to be deciphered. C. S. Lewis made a similar point: 'Nature cannot satisfy the desires she arouses nor answer theological questions.'[4] But nature doesn't tell us what its own true meaning is. As Chesterton pointed out, 'one must somehow find a way of loving the world without trusting it.' For Chesterton, that 'way of loving the world' is provided by Christian doctrine, which allows him to value nature as a pointer to God even when it might seem to witness more to a cosmic lack of meaning, purpose and justice.

The beauty of the creation thus echoes the greater beauty of God. This world may only be a scaled-down version of something greater, but we sometimes catch fragments of the melodies of the New Jerusalem floating by, as on a passing breeze. Perhaps nothing can fully prepare us for heaven when we finally enter it, but we can meditate on the thought that it will be like the very best of this world, only better.

Let's now look at some classic ways in which Christians have understood the notion of creation, and see how they illuminate our thinking about God and the world.

Discerning wisdom: works of art and the creation

One of my memories of my time as an undergraduate at Wadham College, Oxford, is admiring the portrait of Sir Christopher Wren (1632–1723) that adorned the panelled walls of the college's dining hall. It was a particularly fine work of art and I often found myself gazing at it at mealtimes. Wren was a student at Wadham College before going on to achieve considerable renown as an architect. In 1666 the Great Fire of London badly damaged the original St Paul's Cathedral, and a decision was taken to commission a new building. Wren's fame ensured he was selected as the designer, and the current St Paul's, completed in 1710, remains one of London's most famous landmarks.

As it is close to my place of work in central London, I often visit the cathedral to soak up its beauty and elegance. It's hard not to appreciate the superb architectural vision that lies behind the building. Why, though, many visitors wonder, is there no obvious memorial to Wren who is buried in the cathedral? Surely he deserves some recognition!

The fact is that the cathedral itself is a memorial to Wren. On a circle of black marble on the main floor beneath the centre of the dome, visitors will find a Latin inscription that includes the words: 'Reader, if you are looking for a memorial, look around you.'[5] Wren's wisdom and skill are best appreciated not through any kind of eulogy but by studying the masterpiece he created. The creator's genius is seen in the creation itself. Instead of wading through learned tomes about Wren, we are invited to admire his achievement and appreciate his brilliance for ourselves. Of course, an accessible guide book would help us get more out of our exploration of the cathedral, but it would only supplement, never displace, our first-hand encounter with Wren's architectural masterwork.

In a similar way, theology supplements our understanding of God: sometimes it corrects our perceptions, sometimes it enlarges our appreciation of what we experience. But theology must never to be thought of as an alternative for an encounter with God – through prayer, through worship, through reflecting on Scripture or through enjoying God's wonderful creation. There is nothing sadder than a bookish theologian whose somewhat limited knowledge of God is picked up second hand from theology textbooks.

Looking at what God has made always trumps reading books about God. Writers of the European Renaissance knew this and developed a way of ensuring that theological reflection and aesthetic appreciation could be held together. They argued that God had written two 'books' – the Bible and the natural world – using different languages, both of which could be read and understood by human beings. The 'written book' of the Bible helped its readers make sense of God and the world. The 'book of nature' permitted God's wisdom and beauty to be appreciated. The two books were understood to be complementary, allowing God's wisdom in creation to be both *understood* and *experienced*.

The simple truth is that many people find theology textbooks hopelessly dull, but they often experience a sense of awe at the vastness of the universe, and delight in its beauty. The American poet Walt Whitman (1819–92) tells in his poem, 'When I heard the learn'd astronomer', how he found himself bored to distraction by an astronomy lecture. It was all about dull charts and diagrams. Leaving the lecture hall, he went outside into the night and found himself thrilled and overwhelmed as he 'look'd up in perfect silence at the stars'. Theory is dull; reality is brilliant. It's a point C. S. Lewis appreciated, quoting with pleasure from Goethe's *Faust*: 'Theory is grey, but the golden tree of life is green.'

A second way of thinking about the relation of God to creation is to suggest that God is like an artist painting a picture or a writer creating a novel. We often speak of an artist 'putting something of himself' into a painting or a novelist telling a story that is profoundly shaped by her own experience and concerns. Both the painting and the novel are works of art in themselves, which nevertheless convey something of the character and wisdom of their creators. (It is not surprising that book festivals have become so important in recent years, given that they allow people who admire particular novels to encounter and express their appreciation to those who created them.)

One of the finest explorations of this point comes from the pen of Dorothy L. Sayers (1893–1957), whom we met in the first volume of this series. Sayers rose to fame in the 1930s due to the popularity of her books about Lord Peter Wimsey, a flamboyant aristocratic detective whose flair in solving crimes committed in London society gained him a huge readership. As well as being a crime writer, Sayers was a lay theologian and ranked with C. S. Lewis as one of England's finest religious writers of the 1940s. In *The Mind of the Maker* (1941) she drew parallels between God's creation of the world and a novelist's creation of a literary masterpiece.

The Mind of the Maker is a landmark book and of interest for many reasons, not least its reflections on the doctrine of the Trinity (to which we shall turn in the next chapter).

Its most notable aspect, however, is the way it explores the question of why anyone would want to write or create anything in the first place. What reason had God for creating the world? Why does an author write a book? What kind of motivation is involved? Sayers draws on her own experience as a novelist to explore the relation between a writer and her creations, with particular reference to the character of Lord Peter Wimsey.[6]

> The creator's love for his work is not a greedy possessiveness; he never desires to subdue his work to himself but always to subdue himself to his work. The more genuinely creative he is, the more he will want his work to develop in accordance with its own nature, and to stand independent of himself.

Sayers uses the analogy for God creating the world of an author writing a novel to explore and affirm two themes that have been of major importance in Christian thinking. First, creation is a work of *love*. Sayers here sums up the wisdom of the Christian tradition down the ages. Love is the motivation for God's creation of the world. The creation is the expression of God's fundamental character. It is about bringing into being something that is valuable, something that really matters. Yes, it expresses the mind of its creator; but it is also something that is important in its own right. It matters partly because it is not identical with its creator, possessing instead its own distinct God-given identity.

Second, the creation has its own distinct integrity. It originates from God and reflects God's nature and character, but it is different from God. Sayers explores this point by asking us to imagine how an author creates and develops a character in a novel. Unless she respects the integrity of a character, he is likely to remain a two-dimensional and unreal fictional invention that readers will find difficult to take seriously.

Sayers gives an example to make this point. She asks us to imagine a well-intentioned fan of the Lord Peter Wimsey novels suggesting a plotline for a new addition to the series. 'Couldn't you make Lord Peter go to the Antarctic and investigate a murder on an exploring expedition?' Sayers's response is simple. There is no way that Wimsey would do anything of the sort – he isn't like that. He has his own identity and she, the author, has had to work with it. Having created Wimsey with his own 'proper nature', the artist in her simply could not violate the integrity of her creation in such a capricious and arbitrary way.[7]

> Although the writer's love is verily a jealous love, it is a jealousy for and not of his creatures. He will tolerate no interference either with them or between them and himself. But he does not desire that the creature's identity should be merged in his own, nor that his miraculous power should be invoked to wrest the creature from its proper nature.

It's important to appreciate where Sayers's analogy leads. Sometimes people can give the impression that if they were responsible for the world, it would run much better. You probably know the kind of person I have in mind. Once at a meeting I attended, a gentleman complained loudly about how long a project was taking. 'Now let's be reasonable,' our well-meaning chairman responded, 'after all, Rome wasn't built in a day.' 'Well, I wasn't in charge of that job', replied his critic. He knew best.

It's the same with armchair philosophers. Anyone, they tell us, could make a better universe than this one! It would be easy to have a world in which there was no evil – you just need to put the right person in charge of the project. They could deny human beings free will and programme them so they only act in certain ways – and the problem of evil would be sorted out very quickly!

Sayers's approach helpfully exposes the weakness of this somewhat immodest suggestion, which is completely out of tune with the character of God. God creates human beings in order that we might be loved and that we might love God. Love is an act of free response – on our part and on God's. It makes no sense to say that all the world's problems would be solved if we were denied free will. Maybe some would, but humanity would be stripped of its dignity and responsibility, both of which are intrinsic to our creation 'in the image of God' (Genesis 1.27). The rewriting of the human narrative proposed by our well-meaning objector would take us into unchartered territory and tell an entirely different story. Most disastrously, it would deny us the possibility of loving God.

We need to explore the important idea of bearing the 'image of God' in more detail if we are to appreciate this point properly.

Humanity as the bearer of the image of God

At least three ways of thinking about our identity, role and place in the greater scheme of things are opened up when we consider that we bear 'the image of God'.

In the first place, this statement of the origins of humanity reminds us that we are accountable to God. It was a custom in the ancient near East for rulers to display images of themselves throughout their kingdoms – a practice echoed in the golden statue of Nebuchadnezzar (Daniel 3.1–7). These images reminded people of the authority of the ruler over his kingdom. His subjects were under his authority and were accountable to him. One possible way of understanding the idea of being created in the 'image of God' is that it reminds us that we are *accountable to God*.

We find this idea hinted at during an incident in the ministry of Jesus of Nazareth (Luke 20.22–25). When he was challenged about whether it was right for Jews to pay taxes to the Roman authorities, Jesus responded by asking to be shown a denarius – a coin used throughout the Roman Empire that was stamped with an image of the emperor. He asked the crowd to tell him 'whose head and whose title' was stamped on the coin. Those standing around responded that it was Caesar's. Jesus then replied that we must give to Caesar what is Caesar's and to God what is God's. Some might see this as ducking the question, but it's not. It is a superb way of getting us to ask ourselves whose image we bear. And if we bear God's image, are we dedicating ourselves to God?

A second way of understanding the 'image of God' is to see it as pointing to some kind of resonance between divine and human rationality. Because we bear God's image we can discern God's handiwork within the created order – our thinking chimes in with something deeper. There is a surprising degree of harmony between the structures of the world and human reason – but why? Why, for example, does mathematics describe the world so well? After all, mathematical equations are meant to be the free creations of the human mind. Could it be that our patterns of thought are shaped in a way that allows us to discern God's finger-prints within the created order? This idea is found in the opening chapters of Paul's letter to the Romans, which argue that everyone has some basic intuition of the existence of God. It's as if we have a homing instinct that helps us recognize God's presence within the creation.

A third way suggests that to bear the 'image of God' is to have the potential to enter into a relationship with God. God has created humanity with a specific goal – namely to love God and be loved by God. This insight is expressed in Augustine of Hippo's famous prayer to God: 'You have made us for yourself, and our heart is restless until it finds its rest in you.'[8] Human beings only achieve their true identity, goal and meaning when they relate to God.

In recent years the word 'humanism' has been hijacked by those promoting what is actually a 'secular humanism' based on a rather dogmatic anti-religious or atheist worldview. The real meaning of the term 'humanism' is, however, very different: it is about enabling human beings to achieve their full potential. *Christian* humanism – the phrase is not a self-contradiction – is a philosophy of life that holds that, to be truly human, we need to relate to God. I am often invited to debate the 'question of God' with secular humanists, and have found that they are baffled when I tell them I'm a humanist as well – except that I stand in the noble tradition of humanism going back to leading Renaissance thinkers like Erasmus of Rotterdam or Thomas More, who realized that knowing and loving God endowed human life with new dignity and meaning.

Though our brief reflections have, thus far, only scratched the surface of a Christian understanding of human nature (we will reflect further on sin and on human freedom, especially in relation to divine grace, in the fourth volume of this series, *Spirit of the Living God*), we have learned enough to appreciate how important a *right* understanding of human nature is to the Christian life. It provides us with a map with three main reference points.

First, there is our relationship with God. This is something that needs to be sustained through prayer and worship and safeguarded in times when we are busy or under stress. It is surprisingly easy for us to allow other things to displace God – even if only temporarily. Second, there are our relationships with other people. We must learn to see others as bearing God's image and therefore deserving of our respect. Much Christian thinking on issues such as human rights and political liberty rests on this notion, as does the Declaration of Independence (1776) of the United States of America, which is ultimately grounded in a doctrine of creation.

> We hold these truths to be self-evident, that all men are created equal, that they are endowed by their Creator with certain unalienable Rights, that among these are Life, Liberty and the pursuit of Happiness.

Third, we have responsibilities towards the remainder of God's creation. Christianity affirms that we, as human beings, are part of the created order. This does not mean we are on the same level as other elements of the natural world (like puddles of water, blades of grass or sparrows), for human beings are not *indistinguishable* from the rest of creation. Rather, we have been set a little lower than God and 'crowned . . . with glory and honour' (Psalm 8.5). The biblical tradition uses a variety of images to express the idea that human beings have been invested with responsibility for the stewardship of the natural world, and the theme of caring for God's creation is an integral aspect of any Christian environmental ethic.

Creation as a process: God's ongoing involvement with the world

Like many, I enjoy the famous story that lies behind the creation of the great statue of David by the artist Michelangelo (1475–1564). In the late fifteenth century, the Florentine sculptor Agostino d'Antonio began to carve a huge block of marble, hoping to produce a spectacular work. But everything seemed to go wrong, and after a few attempts he discarded the marble, regarding it as worthless. Badly disfigured, it lay idle for 40 years. Then Michelangelo, feeling sure that he could form a magnificent statue out of the abandoned stone, began work. The final piece is widely regarded as one of the most outstanding artistic achievements of all time. The idea was in Michelangelo's mind; his genius lay in transferring it to the real world. He created something expressing his artistic vision.

To speak about 'creating' suggests forming or fashioning something that leaps from the mind of its creator into existence. There is no doubt that this is part of the Christian understanding of creation. God causes the universe to come into being; the world around us owes its origins to God; and the wisdom of God can be seen in the world.

Most of us think about creation as an act. One moment something is not there; the next it is. Back in 1988 I was studying a late medieval manuscript in one of the finest libraries in Paris, the Bibliothèque Nationale. After a hard morning's work I went for a walk to clear my head, crossing one of the many bridges that span the River Seine. Along the riverside there were artists' stalls where you could buy sketches and watercolours of Parisian scenes. Some of the artists were drawing passers-by, who sat posing on canvas chairs. I watched a plain sheet of paper turn into a striking likeness of an old man – one moment the sheet was blank, then a picture appeared.

It's not surprising that many people find it helpful to think of God as an artist or craftsman. To explore this point let's look at a famous image developed by William Paley (1743–1805). Writing in the first years of the nineteenth century when the Industrial Revolution was under way in England, Paley argued that God was like a watchmaker and the world like a watch God had created.[9] Paley took great pleasure in describing the component parts of this wonderful piece of machinery, such as its springs and cogwheels, and suggested that its complex workings helped us, by analogy, to realize how carefully God had designed and constructed the world.

Paley believed that God created the world in its completed form. Just as the watch was constructed, wound up and kept going without need of further attention because it was supremely well made, so, having created the world, God stood back from it and left it to its own devices. God became absent from the creation.

This does not, however, fit with the biblical idea of God as an ongoing presence within a world that matters to God profoundly. The Christian tradition has always insisted that God created the world out of love, so why should God stop loving the world after bringing it into being? Surely God's love of the creation is better expressed in a continuing care for and involvement with it, and a passionate commitment to its good?

Earlier we noticed that the Bible makes use of fatherly and motherly images for God. Let's agree that parents are responsible for bringing their children into being in the first place. But their responsibilities don't end there of course. They have to help their children grow up; they need to be there for them, encouraging and supporting them; they must try to provide an environment in which they can learn to cope with life's problems and fend for themselves. What sort of parents would abandon their children at birth, leaving them to face life on their own?

The Bible often depicts the love of God for the creation in rich and deeply moving ways. The following great passage speaks poignantly of God's love for the people of Israel.

> When Israel was a child, I loved him,
>   and out of Egypt I called my son.
> The more I called them,
>   the more they went from me;
> they kept sacrificing to the Baals,
>   and offering incense to idols.
> Yet it was I who taught Ephraim to walk,
>   I took them up in my arms;
>   but they did not know that I healed them.
> I led them with cords of human kindness,
>   with bands of love.
> I was to them like those
>   who lift infants to their cheeks.
>   I bent down to them and fed them.
>   (Hosea 11.1–4)

Yet, despite God's constant love, Israel chooses to go its own way. God did not create a slave people, to do as they were bidden. He created a people who, if they wished, could turn their backs on their creator. As we shall see later in this series, the Christian doctrine of redemption concerns how God sets out to recall and redirect a wayward and fallen world.

Paley's watchmaking God bears no relation to this loving God so vividly depicted by Hosea. Paley's God has downed tools and gone home. Indeed, some of Paley's more unkind critics suggested that his idea of God as a kind of celestial mechanic was so irrelevant to everyday life that God could retire or die and it would make no difference to anyone. Mainline Christianity thinks of God in a somewhat different way. God is committed to the creation, sustaining it as an expression of love and care. God is not an absentee father who is too busy with other things to bother about those he is meant to love!

The idea of God's fatherly and motherly love therefore plays an essential role in the Christian doctrine of creation, making it clear that creation is not simply a past event, complete in itself, but an ongoing process in which everything grows and develops under the watchful eye of its loving creator. Just as parents provide support and care for their children, so God upholds the creation.

Some might argue that providential care is not normally understood to be part of the process of creation. This is a fair point. Perhaps we need to distinguish between the everyday sense of 'create' and its richer theological meaning. The fact is that when speaking of God's creation of the world, we touch on themes and insights quite absent from everyday language. An analogy may help make this point clearer.

I recall with great pleasure a period of about a week back in 1960 when my school was swept with a craze for making paper planes. We folded sheets of paper in certain ways to create the best models we could. Day after day dozens of us would launch these planes into the air and watch to see whose flew the furthest or stayed in the air the longest. For some reason my planes always seemed to crash ages before anyone else's, but it was still great fun. Eventually the school authorities told us to stop this nonsense: it was creating a massive litter problem; and some of us had discovered that expensive art paper was the best kind for making these planes! But while the craze lasted, my friends and I were in heaven.

Let's linger over a phrase I used when recalling this fond memory: *to 'create' the best models we could*. All we did was take a piece of paper and fold it – a weak interpretation of the word 'create' that just means rearranging or reworking something that already exists. Indeed, some Greek philosophers – such as Plato – argued that creation was really about God reworking material that was already to hand, but Christianity uses the word in a much more sophisticated way. In its fully Christian sense, the idea of creation has two main elements. First, it is about bringing the world into existence. God does not simply impose order and structure on some disorganized material that happens to be lying around, rather God brings the building-blocks of the universe into being, before assembling them to give a regular and ordered universe governed by the 'laws of nature'.

Second, creation is about a process of guiding, upholding and sustaining through which God continues to be present with and within the world. It is no wonder that many theologians argue for the closest of links between the doctrines of creation and providence as they are intricately intertwined.

How might we visualize this second aspect of creation? One of the best ways was worked out by Augustine of Hippo in the first few years of the fifth century. In a commentary on Genesis, Augustine suggests that we think of God as creating a world with lots of dormant seeds. As time passes, God causes these seeds to germinate so that the created order develops, as it is meant to, into something different from its original form.

I have friends who are passionate gardeners. They tell me that creating a garden is about putting a process in place. First you mark out the locations of paths, hedges, areas of grass, rocks and plants. Then when everything is in place and the plants begin to grow you can begin to see what the garden is meant to look like. The designer's vision is only realized after some considerable time!

Augustine's view is that God creates a universe that has the potential to develop over time, so that richer and more complex forms of life may emerge. And just to make sure we don't get the wrong idea, Augustine makes clear that these more complex forms of life don't happen by accident. God's 'seeds', planted within the creation, are expressions of God's will. God keeps an eye on the development of the created order, directing it towards its intended goals. We could say that Augustine thinks of creation having two stages: a 'big bang' in which something totally new comes into being, followed by a process of development over time. Creation originates in the will of God and is to be understood both as an original event and as a continuing process through which God's goodness and love carry on being expressed in the guidance and upholding of the created order.

Creation and science

Christianity understands the universe to be a created reality that is distinct from God yet reveals God's fingerprints at point after point. There is an obvious spiritual lesson here: to study God's creation is to catch glimpses of the beauty and wisdom of the invisible God in the visible world. During the period of the European Renaissance another aspect of the Christian doctrine of creation began to emerge as particularly significant: God had created an ordered universe, which could be described mathematically by the 'laws of nature'.

Since God is the creator and sustainer of nature, then natural processes themselves can be seen as an expression of God's will. Turning to the writings of the leading Christian theologian Thomas Aquinas in the thirteenth century, we find Aquinas declaring that God, who is the cause of all things, created a world with its own ordering and processes. While God is perfectly capable of doing certain things directly, Aquinas argues that God normally chooses to delegate causal efficacy to the created order. God creates a universe governed by a framework of laws and secondary causes, so that its regularity is open to human investigation.

This idea played a leading role in the Scientific Revolution in Western Europe. The great astronomer Johannes Kepler (1571–1630) noted that the 'laws of nature' seemed to reflect basic geometrical principles. And since geometry had its origins in the mind of God, he suggested, it was only to be expected that the created order would reflect these ideas:

> Since geometry is part of the divine mind from the origins of time, even from before the origins of time . . . it has provided God with the patterns for the creation of the world, and has been transferred to humanity with the 'image of God'.[10]

Many historians have suggested that a Christian doctrine of creation provided the essential background for the emergence of the natural sciences. It's hard to prove this, as we would have to be able to replay history to check it out, but it makes a lot of sense. For a start, Christianity provides a religious motivation for the study of nature – meditating on what God has made enables us to appreciate God all the more.

Christianity also emphasizes the regularity of the natural world, which is not haphazard and random but given order by God.

Christianity thus has no quarrel with science. Indeed, scientific successes can be seen as an indirect confirmation of Christianity's big picture. But we have every right to criticize science when it starts behaving as if it's a religion or declares that it has 'disproved' God's existence. It has achieved nothing of the sort, and in any case lacks the intellectual equipment to do so. It's no wonder so many scientists are alarmed at the way militant atheists have hijacked science in their war against religion – it's given science a bad name.

The natural sciences regularly throw up important questions about the meaning of life that are beyond the capacity of the scientific method to answer. It is important to appreciate that there are different 'levels of meaning' in the world: science answers questions at one level; Christianity at another – and both answers need to be held together if we are to have a comprehensive understanding of our purpose and place in the universe.

It's well worth exploring this concept that we can offer different levels of explanation for something. Imagine you are walking along a country road and you see two people ahead of you. They've stopped. The man raises his arm, and points. What's going on? On a physiological level, the man's brain has sent signals through his nervous system that have caused certain muscles to contract and his arm to move. That's part of, but not the full, picture – it doesn't tell us *why* the man raised his arm and pointed; it confuses mechanism with meaning.

In fact the man had seen a hawk in the sky and wanted to point it out to his companion. That's another level of explanation – it's not inconsistent with the first level but adds to it, giving a fuller account of what was going on. In real life we need many levels of explanation to make sense of things. Science offers one, but there are others, which help us gain a fuller picture.

Imagine you're listening to your favourite piece of music. You could give a good scientific explanation of what you're hearing in terms of patterns of vibrations, but this won't help you understand why you like it so much or why it never fails to lift your mood. Similarly, there is far more to a great painting than an analysis of its chemical components or the physical arrangement of its elements. With both music and art we need to weave in additional levels of explanation to understand what's really going on.

Now that you've got used to this way of thinking, let's ask a simple question: why are we here? At a scientific level we can give a reasonably good account of the processes and factors that lead to the existence of life. That answers the 'how' level, but there's a deeper aspect – the 'why' level. Most scientists would say that science can't answer that deeper question – and they're right. Science can tell us how we came to be here but it can't tell us why.

The Christian faith complements science. It adds levels of explanation that science cannot access. The scientist tells us that the contemporary scientific understanding of how the universe came into being is that it did so through the big bang. The Christian agrees with this and adds something extra – namely, that this fits into the Christian doctrine of creation, which allows us to speak of the universe having meaning and purpose.

In this chapter we have emphasized how Christianity is able to make sense of things, especially within the created order. We now need to move on to an aspect of the Christian understanding of God that leaves many Christians uneasy: the doctrine of the Trinity. Why encumber a simple faith with such a complicated idea that seems to make little sense?

In the next chapter, we will begin to find out.

5

Mystery or muddle? The Trinity

When I was an atheist I regarded religious people as deluded and irrational souls who believed all sorts of ridiculous nonsense. If I had been asked to single out what I regarded as the most absurd aspect of Christian belief, I would have pointed to the doctrine of the Trinity. How can God be three and one at the same time? It was simply gibberish, on the same level as the ideas of one of P. G. Wodehouse's most brilliant literary creations, the empty-headed Madeline Bassett – a passionate advocate of the belief that 'the stars are God's daisy chain' or that 'every time a fairy blows its wee nose a baby is born'.

When I discovered Christianity as a student, I began to explore the landscape of faith. It was an exciting and reward-ing process and I found I was able to make sense of a lot of basic Christian ideas quite quickly. But the doctrine of the Trinity still seemed quite irrational. I asked some local clergy to explain it to me. Perhaps I was unlucky or unwise, but it soon became obvious to me that they had as little understanding as I did.

I decided I was basically faced with two choices. The one I feared to be the more sensible – to judge by the muddled and incoherent (but doubtless well-meaning) responses I got from several ordained ministers – was that this doctrine really made no sense at all and that I would eventually discover this was the case. Yet I knew the Trinity had been taken very seriously by leading Christian thinkers of the past – people I was now learning to respect. Maybe when I had learned more, the pieces would fall into place.

So fearing the first and hoping for the second, I kept thinking about the matter when I began to study theology seriously in 1976. By the time I left Oxford to go to Cambridge for further studies in 1978, I was firmly convinced that the doctrine of the Trinity did indeed make sense. In exploring this aspect of the landscape of faith, I had worried I would become lost in a dark and lifeless wilderness. In fact I entered a verdant garden of delight, and in this chapter I will share the insights that led me to embrace and affirm what I had once approached with trepidation and anxiety.

Let's begin by making a point that's essential to a right understanding of this issue.

Why we can't reduce God to neat little formulae

I began to love science at about the age of ten and eagerly tried to absorb scientific works that I now realize were far too advanced for me. At the age of thirteen I plucked up the courage to ask one of my teachers to explain Einstein's theory of relativity. He loaned me one of his books to read, and a week later we met for half an hour to talk about it. I'll never forget how the conversation ended. 'You're not ready for this just yet. Your brain needs to grow before you'll be able to take it in. We'll talk again in five years' time.' Some might think my teacher was being patronizing, but I found what he said wise, encouraging and, above all, realistic.

We never had that later conversation, partly because I worked out the theory of relativity for myself about two years later. But the point my teacher made was right: my mind needed to expand before I could make sense of Einstein. It's no accident that some of the ancient Greek philosophers talk about education as *psychagogia* – an 'enlargement of the soul'. My problem as a thirteen year old was that I was trying to reduce reality to what I could then cope with. Unfortunately for me, reality was somewhat bigger!

When we're confronted with a concept that's just too great for us to take in, our natural instinct is to scale it down to something more manageable – we leave out the complicated bits or we simplify it by pretending it's really something different. There's nothing wrong with that – unless we think our scaled-down version of reality is the way things really are. But, of course, it isn't. What we're doing in making something simple is leaving out the complicated parts or forcing something complex into a little box and throwing away the bits that don't fit. Simplification is always about reduction – and sometimes about distortion as well.

Similarly, we can't fit God into a neat little slogan. A theory about God is never going to capture God's radiance, beauty or wonder. Mr Beaver's remark about Aslan in *The Lion, the Witch and the Wardrobe* applies with even greater force to God: 'He's wild, you know. Not like a tame lion.' We cannot domesticate God, who is supremely resistant to our attempts to reduce reality to our level. When Paul declares that the peace of God 'surpasses all understanding' (Philippians 4.7) he is not suggesting such peace is irrational. Rather, he is conceding that the human mind simply cannot comprehend the enormity of God's love and grace. It's too big for us to take in properly – or express fully in words.

Augustine of Hippo offered one of the finest accounts of the limits of our ability to capture God in neat formulae. If you can get your mind around it, he remarked, it's not God – it's something else you might incorrectly think is God. Anything we can grasp fully and completely *cannot* be God, precisely because it would be so limited and impoverished. Instead of trying to reduce God to our own level we ought to be trying to expand our minds to take in as much of God as possible – and that's going to cause us mental discomfort. The only way we can avoid this mental pain, as we've seen, is by reducing God to our level. But it's not God we're thinking about any more, rather we've simply created a god in our own likeness – a self-serving human invention that may bear some passing similarity to God but falls far short of the glory and majesty of the God who created and redeemed the world.

There's a story about Augustine that makes this point rather nicely. Augustine was bishop of Hippo Regius, a Roman coastal town in North Africa. While writing his major work, *On the Trinity*, he decided to take a break and went for a stroll along the beautiful beaches nearby. As he walked he came across a young boy behaving rather strangely. Over and over again the boy went to the edge of the shoreline, filled a container full of seawater then emptied this into a hole he had dug in the beach.

Augustine watched this for some time, mystified. What was going on? Eventually he decided to ask. The boy pointed to the Mediterranean Sea and said, 'I am going to empty the ocean into this hole in the sand.' Augustine probably smiled, in that rather pained way that reflects amusement at the strange and naive ideas of younger people. 'You can't do that! You'll never fit the ocean into that tiny hole you've dug.' The boy supposedly replied: 'And you're wasting your time writing a book about God. You'll never fit God into a book!'

Now there are some very awkward questions about the historical reliability of this story but, true or not, it makes a point that must be uppermost in our minds as we try to wrestle with God. In the end our minds just aren't big enough to cope with God – God simply overwhelms our mental capacities, as the midday sun dazzles our eyes if we are unwise enough to stare at it.

We have to get used to the limits placed on our under-standing of things. Many years ago I read a biography of Galileo Galilei (1564–1642), the great Italian astronomer. The part that really excited me was the description of his discovery of the four moons of the planet Jupiter. These can't be seen with the naked eye, but Galileo was able to use a telescope to vastly aid his vision. Over the period 1609–10 he was able to observe the moons now known as Io, Europa, Ganymede and Callisto, and track their orbits around the distant planet.

Now suppose that telescopes had never been invented. We would be limited to what the human eye could see unaided, and the vast riches of the universe that modern astronomy has uncovered would have remained unknown to us. They were always there but we were just unable to perceive them – we needed help to extend the range of our natural vision in order to grasp the astonishing complexity of the universe in which we live. The moons of Jupiter didn't suddenly come into existence because someone finally saw them; they were there all the time. The problem was that they lay beyond the range of human vision.

God exceeds what our minds can cope with in much the same way as the physical universe so vastly exceeds what we can see on our own. What we do perceive is real and reliable; it's just that, in spiritual terms, our vision is limited, 'For now we see in a mirror, dimly' (1 Corinthians 13.12). Our eyes need to be opened, and our sight healed, if we are to see God properly.

The doctrine of the Trinity is the outcome of the Christian community's principled stand against reducing God to a level we can cope with. It aims to tell the truth about God, no matter how difficult we find this to take in. We think we're doing God a favour; in reality we're just making ourselves the 'measure of all things' (to use a phrase from the pre-Socratic philosopher Protagoras). We try to reduce God to what we can cope with; instead God wants to expand our minds.

The Christian story of salvation: doing justice to God

The Christian Church has always realized that getting God right trumps everything. The doctrine of the Trinity aims to integrate all the elements of the rich and complex biblical witness to the character and deeds of God into the Christian story of salvation. Let's focus on three great interwoven themes: first, the transcendent God who brings this world into existence; second, the God who becomes incarnate and redeems the world in and through Jesus of Nazareth; and third, the God who is present in history and experience, and whom we encounter through the Holy Spirit. *The fundamental insight we need to grasp is that the entire story is about the one and the same God.*

God isn't like a sheriff in the days of the Wild West, who deputized homesteaders to help with law enforcement. God doesn't entrust the precious work of creation and redemption to underlings or surrogates. No – everything that needs to be done is done by the one and the same God. And reflecting on the works of God helps us understand and appreciate more about this God – insights that are summed up (though not explained!) in the concept of the Trinity.

So how best are we to express this rich and wonderful vision of God in a way that is relevant to today's culture? Some find the traditional formula, 'Father, Son and Holy Spirit', rather too masculine. We need to recall, of course, that God is *above* gender – God creates male and female yet is neither male nor female. It's tricky to speak of personal realities when we're limited to gendered language, and quite easy to assume, in any case, that a person, capable of entering into a relationship, must be either a 'he' or a 'she'. But just because that's true of humans it doesn't mean it's true of God as well. The doctrine of the Trinity reminds us that God stands outside this linguistic limitation. God relates to us without being a 'he' or 'she', and though our language struggles to cope with this insight, we must somehow find a way of dealing with it.

Some try to avoid the problem by speaking of the Trinity as creator, redeemer and sustainer. This may get round the gender issue[1] but it creates a new and worrying problem: it adopts a functionalist approach to God and loses sight of the more fundamental theme of relationship. It's almost like a bureaucratic 'job description' for God, whereas so many of the great themes of the Christian vision of God – love, mercy, faithfulness – find their natural context in a loving and trusting relationship.

What of the formula 'three persons but one substance'? This has traditionally been used to safeguard the richness of our experience of God on the one hand and the certain fact that there is only one God on the other. There is one divine reality (the 'substance') but God's richness is expressed in the three persons. We may focus on each of the persons individually but this will only help us appreciate the one God even better. Back in the fifth century, Augustine of Hippo pointed out that the vocabulary of the Trinity seems ill adapted to deal with its subject. We have to talk about 'persons' and 'substance', he suggested, because that's the way things are – but the terms aren't ideal.

For many, as for my younger self, the main difficulty with the doctrine of the Trinity is its apparent illogicality. How can we speak of one God in three persons? Let's adapt the Christian narrative idea we discussed above a little, and think of the sweep of salvation as a great drama with three roles or parts: one role is creating the world; the second is redeeming it through Jesus Christ; the third is the ongoing presence of God in the life of the believer and the Church through the Holy Spirit. We naturally tend to think of each of these roles – creator, redeemer and sustainer – being played by a different actor or agent. The doctrine of the Trinity, however, declares that God isn't reduced to any one of these roles – the one and the same God plays all three parts.

What if we simplified this and reduced it to something we could manage more easily? Let's pretend God is just creator – it's a classic idea of God we find in ancient Greek philosophy: God made the world, constructed and wound up the great cosmic clock and then left it to fend for itself. There's nothing complicated about this – but that's because it leaves out any mention of the rich and complex presence and action of God in history.

And that's a big problem: this neat little way of thinking about God leaves out much that's integral to the Christian vision of God; a long and glorious drama has been reduced to a single act. What about redemption? What about God's ongoing presence in our lives? We've not told the full story; in fact we've ended up with an impoverished and distorted view of God that bears little relation to what we discover in the Bible, the creeds or the life of the Church.

In this view God is a distant creator who never becomes directly involved in our world's affairs – God governs from the safety of heaven, far removed from the problems and dangers we face, rather like a general directing his front-line troops from the safety of a bomb-proof bunker. And Christians *know* God just isn't like that – God entered into this world in Jesus of Nazareth: 'the Word became flesh and lived among us, and we have seen his glory' (John 1.14).

I have a professional interest in the development of Christian theology. As I look at Christian attempts to represent God down the ages I can see a tension between two desires. One is to do justice to the way God actually is; the other to represent God simply and accessibly. I sympathize with both, but since the human mind struggles – and ultimately fails – to cope with the majesty and brilliance of God, there is really only one way forward. Instead of limiting God to what reason can cope with we need to expand our minds to try to take God in – and that's often best done in the context of prayer and worship rather than rational reflection.

Of course we want to make things simple – who doesn't – but simplification easily leads to reduction and reduction to distortion, which is just not acceptable. Good theology is about doing justice to God and feeling the pain as our frail and feeble minds try to wrap themselves around divine reality. Our misgivings about the Trinity arise mainly because this reality does not map easily on to our natural categories of thought – we have to accept that the Trinity is in a category of its own.

The theologians of the early Church gave careful thought to all their intellectual options in formulating a properly Christian doctrine of God. They wanted it to be simple; they also wanted it to be authentic and reliable. To put it very crudely: they realized that if the Son and Holy Spirit are not God in the same sense as the Father, we cannot be saved; nor can we know God properly and fully. In a way, the doctrine of the Trinity doesn't solve any problems, but it does stop us making mistakes – serious mistakes – about the Christian understanding of God. That's why the great Swiss theologian Emil Brunner (1889–1966) was right when he argued that the Trinity is a 'security doctrine', designed to protect the glory and majesty of God from our well-meaning attempts to scale these down to something easier for us to handle.

Let's make a helpful distinction here. What is the difference between a *puzzle* and a *mystery*? Austin Farrer (1904–68), a colleague of C. S. Lewis at Oxford University, used this distinction a lot – as his wife was a noted author of crime fiction, it came naturally to him.[2] Farrer realized that most detective novels are really puzzles rather than mysteries – once you have enough information there's nothing to stop you solving the puzzle and producing a nice neat answer. Providing you piece it together properly, a good detective novel allows you to work out the identity of the murderer through cool and clinical logic. So a puzzle is a problem we can solve if we can get some more information.

But not every problem, Farrer argued, was a puzzle. Some were mysteries lying beyond the ability of the human mind to grasp. So what stops us from grasping a mystery properly? Why can't we solve it? Farrer insisted it was not a lack of information but something more fundamental: our minds simply weren't big enough to take in these mysteries. There were no slick and neat solutions here – we catch glimpses of possible solutions but they always seem to lie beyond our reach. Puzzles lead to logical answers; mysteries often force us to stretch language to its limits in an attempt to describe a reality just too great to take in properly.

It's easy to see how this distinction helps us think about the Trinity. It's not a puzzle, it's a mystery – it's not something we can dissect using cool logic. As the prophet Isaiah discovered in his vision in the Jerusalem temple (Isaiah 6.1–8), the experience of God is overwhelming, transcending our ability to describe or capture it in all its glory and majesty. Farrer simply asks us to realize there are limits to our understanding. A failure to understand something does not mean it is irrational; it may simply mean it lies on the far side of our limited abilities to take things in and make complete sense of them. And that's the way things are with the doctrine of the Trinity. A great God leads to a profound doctrine.

Going deeper into reality:
the Trinity and 'surface faith'

Now some will read these words and rightly wish to raise an objection. Their faith is simple; and they like it that way. They trust in God and believe firmly that they've been redeemed through Christ, so why do they need to believe this complicated stuff about the Trinity? Isn't their simple faith good enough? Some people think the Trinity is basically a note in small print added to a simple account of God, making things inconveniently complicated. These are reasonable concerns and they deserve a thoughtful answer.

No, you don't *need* to believe in the Trinity; but when you start to reflect on your faith you will find that – maybe without knowing it – you already *do* believe in it. It may not be something you explicitly affirm, but it's implicit in what you already believe. There's a kind of Trinitarian grammar to the way we speak about our faith in God. Let's tease this out a little.

If you're holding a coin in your hand and let it go, it will fall to earth. If you're growing apples or pears in your garden, the fruit will drop off the tree when it's ripe. These are very simple, familiar observations and there's nothing difficult about them. But what is the bigger picture here? Why do things fall to earth in the first place?

Isaac Newton (1642–1727), one of the geniuses of the Scientific Revolution of the seventeenth century, realized that such everyday observations pointed to the existence of something deeper – a force he called 'gravity'. He was able to show that the same general principle that governed apples falling to the ground also applied to planets orbiting the sun. Everyone already knew apples fell off trees – what Newton did was reveal this as part of a bigger picture.

The Trinity is the bigger picture of God that results from teasing out the implications of what we know about God from the Bible and our experience. Christians pray and worship; they talk about being saved by Christ; they talk about being guided by the Holy Spirit. But what concept of God is implicit in these beliefs? What must be true about God if these simple statements of faith are right and reliable?

Let's look at two basic statements that are hard-wired into the Christian faith.

1 Jesus Christ is our saviour.
2 Jesus Christ reveals God.

We're so familiar with these that we don't give them much thought, but what do these seemingly simple statements presuppose? After all, when we explicitly affirm them we implicitly affirm what lies behind them.

It might be helpful to think of Christian faith as being like an iceberg. The visible part comprises the many aspects of faith with which we're very familiar, such as prayer and worship. But the fate of the liner *Titanic* on her maiden voyage in 1912 reminds us that most of an iceberg is unseen – nine-tenths of it is below the waterline, supporting and upholding the small part that is visible.

Let's change the analogy: imagine you come across a lake – perhaps on a country walk or in an ornamental garden – in which water lilies are growing. Or think of the many paintings of water lilies by Claude Monet (1840–1926), based on his garden at Giverny. Their great leaves and elegant flowers seem to float on the surface of the water, creating an impression of tranquillity and harmony. But what is going on below?

In fact the surface appearance is sustained by a complex root system. The water lilies grow on stalks embedded in the ground at the bottom of the pond. These roots provide both physical support and biological nourishment for the leaves and flowers – they're part of a bigger picture not fully apparent to the observer delighting in the delicate ornamental blooms on show.

A 'surface faith' is about what we see and experience. It involves prayer and worship; it's about affirming the articles of the creeds and talking about Jesus of Nazareth as our Saviour and Lord. But beneath this is a 'deep faith' – a set of more profound beliefs implied by our 'surface faith'. The doctrine of the Trinity is like the part of the iceberg under the water. It's there and needs to be there, but for everyday purposes you don't have to worry about it – you can live out the Christian life without explicitly talking about the Trinity! What you must realize is that there is a deep Trinitarian logic to the language of our faith. When we *declare* that 'Jesus is Lord!', we *imply* that God is Trinity.

It's a bit like breathing. We breathe to live and we can do this perfectly well without understanding the chemical composition of the earth's atmosphere, or how the human respiratory process works. The Trinity is the oxygen of Christian faith and life – it upholds us even if we don't realize what it's all about. Yet when we start going deeper into our faith, its full richness and significance begin to unfold before our eyes.

In his winsome study of Francis of Assisi, G. K. Chesterton urged his readers to let their faith be not like a 'theory' but like a 'love-affair'.[3] It's a good point: love is not a 'thing', something we can possess or control; rather, 'God is love' (1 John 4.16), and we are called to love this loving God by participating in a relationship with the one who loved us first. And the more we think about the dynamics of a loving relationship, the more we realize we need to expand our vision of God. You can't love – in the proper sense of that word – an idea! To encounter God is to experience God in the deepest of ways. C. S. Lewis put it like this: 'Hitherto you have experienced truth only with the abstract intellect. I will bring you where you can taste it like honey and be embraced by it as by a bridegroom. Your thirst shall be quenched.'[4]

The Trinity is our attempt to put into words – however faltering and inadequate – the full wonder of this God, who created us, knows us, loves us and enters into history to find and meet us.

Theologians tend to approach the Trinity in two main ways. Some argue that it is the Christian faith's last word about God – it's like the keystone in an arch. When engineers built arches in ancient Rome, they began by constructing a curved wooden frame to hold together the stones. But when the keystone was put in place at the top of the arch, the wooden frame could be taken away – it was the final element of the arch, and once in place held the whole structure together without need of any external support.

That's the view I take. I see the doctrine of the Trinity as the conclusion of a long process of reflection about faith – the keystone in the arch of Christian beliefs, the final piece in the jigsaw. But once you've grasped it it holds everything together. It's like strong glue binding the structure of faith together – or a big picture that makes sense of all the snapshots.

Others argue it's the foundation of faith – instead of being the keystone, it's the cornerstone, around and upon which all the remaining stones are arranged and laid. If this stone is correctly positioned, everything else will fall into place naturally.

But whichever view you decide to take yourself, the important thing to remember is this: you can live in a building without needing to think too much about how it was constructed; we can get on with the Christian life without losing sleep over the fine details of Trinitarian theology! But it helps to know that the building is stable and rests on a secure foundation.

Now, although these ideas are not easy to grasp, many readers will hopefully feel that they are beginning to see the light at the end of the tunnel. To help move things along further, we will turn again to C. S. Lewis and Dorothy L. Sayers.

Getting some help: C. S. Lewis and Dorothy L. Sayers

After an initial period as an atheist, Lewis developed a faith in God in 1930 and moved towards a definite Christian commitment late in 1931. As he began to explore his faith he clearly gave some thought to the idea of the Trinity, as is evident in a letter of 1934 to the American philosopher Paul Elmer More (1864–1937).[5] For Lewis, the doctrine of the Trinity allows us to affirm the transcendence of God without implying that God is 'the immobile, the unanswering'. He believes that 'the huge historic fact of the doctrine of the Trinity' sets out a vision of an eternal and perfect God who enters history as 'a purposing, feeling, and finally crucified Man in a particular place and time'. It is an appropriate and helpful way of expressing the core intuitions about God that lie at the heart of the Christian faith.

Lewis also offers us approaches to the Trinity that allow us to look at this abstract doctrine in a visual way. First of all he makes the point that the doctrine of the Trinity makes sense of the Christian experience of prayer.[6] Imagine an 'ordinary simple Christian' – that is, a believer who would not think of himself or herself as a theologian – kneeling down to pray. What does this Christian experience?

Well, perhaps most obviously, prayer is about getting in touch with God – but as Lewis points out, Christians know it's more complicated than that. For a start it's as if someone is helping us to pray; more than that, it's as if someone is acting as the channel for those prayers.

> You see what is happening. God is the thing to which [the Christian] is praying – the goal he is trying to reach. God is also the thing inside him which is pushing him on – the motive power. God is also the road or bridge along which he is being pushed to that goal. So that the whole threefold life of the three-personal Being is actually going on in that ordinary little bedroom where an ordinary man is saying his prayers.[7]

Lewis's point is that the believer's experience of prayer fits into the big picture provided by the Christian faith. The doctrine chimes in with experience and helps us make more sense of what is going on.

Lewis has two more helpful things to say. First, he reminds his readers that a religious theory or doctrine is always secondary to the reality to which it refers. The doctrine of the Trinity is an attempt to capture the experience of God; it makes no sense in isolation from that experience and can never hope to capture its imaginative or emotional power.

Second, Lewis points out that we see things from a limiting and constrictive human perspective. He suggests that we think of ourselves as 'Flatlanders', two-dimensional people who are trying (and failing!) to visualize three-dimensional objects.

> Flatlanders, attempting to imagine a cube, would either imagine the six squares coinciding, and thus destroy their distinctness, or else imagine them set out side by side, and thus destroy the unity. Our difficulties about the Trinity are of much the same kind.[8]

Lewis doesn't really offer his readers a defence of the doctrine of the Trinity or any new evidence for believing in it. Instead he provides a visual framework that allows us to perceive things in a new way and realize that our previous difficulties arose from seeing them from a limited – and limiting – perspective.

In the previous chapter we began to note some of the themes of Dorothy L. Sayers' *The Mind of the Maker* (1941), which also explores aspects of the doctrine of the Trinity. As an author, Sayers feels there are three distinct stages in the process of creative activity that underlies the writing of a book: the *idea* itself; its *implementation*; the process of *interaction*. She suggests that a book comes into existence first as an ideal construct, built outside time and space but complete in the mind of the author. It is then realized in time and space by pen, ink and paper. The creation is only complete, however, when someone reads the book, thus interacting with the mind of its maker and being transformed by the author's vision.

The mind of the author thus leads initially to the act of writing, then to the experience of reading and comprehending the story, but the process is only complete when the author's idea has entered into a reader's mind. There is a natural progression between what Sayers terms 'Book-as-Thought', 'Book-as-Written' and 'Book-as-Power'. Sayers is making an explicit link between God's self-communication and the doctrine of the Trinity – God is the source of revelation but that revelation takes place in a specific historical form, and needs to be understood and interpreted.

Now some have argued that Sayers's approach is a little too dependent on late-Romantic views of human creativity, and there may be some truth in this. But the points she makes are fair and important. We begin with the idea of a revealing God – a God who has something to say to us. Revelation takes place in an accessible manner, through something we can see and hold. For Sayers it is a book of words; for classical Christianity it is the 'word made flesh', Jesus Christ. God chooses to enter into our world in a form that is understandable to us. Finally, this revelation has the power to take hold of us, capture our imaginations, transform the way we think and live.

In their different ways, then, Lewis and Sayers help us appreciate the inner Trinitarian logic of the Christian faith. What difference does this make to the way we live and think as Christians? In the final section of this chapter we shall consider how the Trinity gives us a lens that allows us to deepen our appreciation of God.

The Trinity and the enrichment of the Christian life

I was invited to give a lecture at Aberystwyth University in north Wales a few years back. How best to get there from Oxford, I wondered? Travelling by train turned out to be a bad idea as I would have to change at least three times, and there was the possibility of delay at several points. So I decided to drive. As it was a long way I consulted a map to work out where to have a break. The best route went through the rural county of Herefordshire, and the areas around several villages were marked on my map as being of 'outstanding natural beauty'. I decided that I would stop at one of those for a cup of tea.

Dining in college the night before my journey, I happened to sit next to a visiting academic who came from somewhere in Herefordshire. I mentioned a few of the villages and asked if he knew them. He did, and had grown up in one of them. 'They're quite nice. Black and white houses. That sort of thing. And there are some nice rivers around.' It seemed like faint praise but I saw no reason to change my plans.

My journey was delightful. It was a sunny day and the villages looked stunningly beautiful. I enjoyed several brisk walks along winding river paths surrounded by lush country-side, and a week later happened to meet my colleague again in the college's Senior Common Room. I told him I had found the villages rather more wonderful than he had led me to expect. He looked a little sheepish. 'Well, I'm not very good with words, you see. And if you grow up there, I suppose you get so used to their beauty that you just take it for granted.'

I valued those words and often mull them over in my mind. We've already talked a lot about how words let us down: they don't seem able to express our feelings of joy and delight – nor, when it comes to it, our sorrow and despair – in the way we would like. But it was the second thing my colleague said that really hit home to me. If you live in a beautiful place for a long time, it becomes ordinary and mundane. I worked in Oxford for many years and still find myself baffled by the large numbers of tourists it attracts, but there is obviously something very special about the city that visitors appreciate immediately on their arrival.

The familiar can all too easily appear dull and ordinary as time progresses. God can become like a comfortable armchair, a well-worn and oft-read book or an old friend – so much a part of us that we lose any sense they are somehow *special*. We forget how they came to be important to us. Every now and then we need to remind ourselves just how wonderful they are.

The doctrine of the Trinity is a wake-up call to do something about our overfamiliarity with God. How? Because it invites us to *rediscover* God. It asks us to think about the world around us – the starry heavens, majestic mountains, verdant pastures and tree-lined rivers. All of these bear witness to the creator God. *But there is more to God than this.*

We are then asked to reflect on Jesus of Nazareth – seeing him not simply as a wonderful human being but also as the word become flesh, as God incarnate in history. And as we think about Jesus of Nazareth, especially his death on the cross, we realize we are dealing with a God who expresses love for us in action; who bears and wears the scars of our pain and suffering; and who gives us hope as we struggle to live out our lives in the world. *But there is more to God than this.*

Finally, we are invited to remember that God is with us now. The God who once breathed life into us can refresh us and renew us. God is in our experience, our prayer and our worship. *But there is more to God than this.*

Focusing individually on the three persons of the Trinity enriches our vision of the one God. This is what the great fourth-century theologian Gregory of Nazianzus was getting at when he wrote: 'As soon as I think of the One, I am illumined by the splendour of the Three; no sooner do I distinguish them than I am carried back to the One.'[9]

Good theology is about expanding (not distorting!) our vision of God as we realize how much we limit God by our preconceptions and misunderstandings. The doctrine of the Trinity helps us recapture the vibrant reality of God in our minds and in our hearts. It liberates us from our scaled-down and domesticated half-truths about a God who can never be confined to formulae or theories.

Those who complain about the 'irrationality' of the Trinity are really people who want to limit reality to what reason can manage. They want to reduce God to what we can cope with or turn God into something we can control. But God cannot be imprisoned, and we ought not to be surprised if the theoretical rationalist cage we have constructed in our minds suddenly breaks into pieces, unable to contain the majesty and glory of a living God! In the end it is God who must be allowed to shape our thinking. The contours of our thought need to be adapted to God, not the other way round!

One of the best ways of sustaining our vision of God is through worship. The doctrine of the Trinity helps us to see that when we worship God through Christ in the Holy Spirit, God has not only prompted us to worship in the first place but is also enabling us to catch a vision of all that God is and all that God has done for us. And as we take in the majesty of God, we end up realizing that the best response to this glorious, living reality is simply to adore.

Moving on

This volume has opened up further themes of the creeds in surveying some of the basic Christian ideas about God. In *Lord and Saviour: Jesus of Nazareth* we shall focus on what is, in many ways, the centrepiece of the Christian faith as we explore more thoroughly what Christians mean when they declare that they 'believe in Jesus Christ'.

Notes

1 Which God are we talking about?

1 He later wrote about this in his autobiography: see Jürgen Moltmann, *A Broad Place: An Autobiography*. Minneapolis, MN: Fortress Press, 2008, 29–33.
2 Moltmann, *A Broad Place*, 30.
3 Moltmann, *A Broad Place*, 30.
4 C. S. Lewis, *Surprised by Joy*. London: HarperCollins, 2002, 265.
5 Lewis, *Surprised by Joy*, 266.
6 Dorothy L. Sayers, *The Mind of the Maker*. London: Methuen, 1941, 16.

2 A personal God: love and faithfulness

1 Mary C. Fjeldstad, *The Thoughtful Reader*. New York: Harcourt Brace College Publishers, 1994, 3.
2 Augustine of Hippo, *Homily on Psalm 119*.
3 Anselm of Canterbury, 'Prayer to St Paul', in *Prayers and Meditations of St Anselm*, trans. Benedicta Ward. Harmondsworth: Penguin, 1973, 153–4.
4 For what follows, see Martin Buber, *I and Thou*, trans. Ronald Gregor Smith. New York: Scribner, 1958. Buber's approach is often referred to as 'dialogical personalism'.
5 C. S. Lewis, *The Four Loves*. London: HarperCollins, 2002, 152–3.
6 See David Keck, *Forgetting Whose We Are: Alzheimer's Disease and the Love of God*. Nashville, TN: Abingdon Press, 1996; John Swinton, *Dementia: Living in the Memories of God*. Grand Rapids, MI: Eerdmans, 2012.

3 An almighty God: power, compassion and suffering

1 Rainer Bucher, *Hitler's Theology: A Study in Political Religion.* London: Continuum, 2011, 58–66.

2 Karl Barth, *Dogmatics in Outline.* London: SCM Press, 1949, 48.

3 Blaise Pascal, *Pensées.* Minneola, NY: Dover, 2003, 77.

4 G. K. Chesterton, *Orthodoxy.* Rockville, MD: Serenity, 2009, 137.

5 Chesterton, *Orthodoxy*, 138.

6 C. S. Lewis, *Mere Christianity.* London: HarperCollins, 2002, 38.

7 C. S. Lewis, *The Problem of Pain.* London: HarperCollins, 2002, 91.

8 Lewis, *Problem of Pain*, xii.

9 Letter to Warnie Lewis, 3 December 1939, in *The Collected Letters of C. S. Lewis*; 3 vols. London: HarperCollins, 2000–6, vol. 2, 302.

10 C. S. Lewis, *A Grief Observed*, New York: HarperCollins, 1994, 44.

4 Creator of heaven and earth

1 G. K. Chesterton, *Orthodoxy.* Rockville, MD: Serenity, 2009, 67.

2 Helge Kragh, *Conceptions of Cosmos: From Myths to the Accelerating Universe – A History of Cosmology.* Oxford: Oxford University Press, 2007.

3 Chesterton, *Orthodoxy*, 66.

4 C. S. Lewis, *The Four Loves.* London: HarperCollins, 2002, 26–7.

5 The full Latin text reads: SUBTUS CONDITOR HUIUS ECCLESIÆ ET VRBIS CONDITOR CHRISTOPHORUS WREN, QUI VIXIT ANNOS ULTRA NONAGINTA, NON SIBI SED BONO PUBLICO. LECTOR SI MONUMENTUM REQUIRIS CIRCUMSPICE. Obijt xxv Feb: An:° MDCCXXIII Æt: xci. 'Here lies the creator of this church and city, Christopher Wren, who lived beyond ninety years, not for

his own but for the public good. Reader, if you are looking for a memorial, look around you. Died 25 February in the year 1723, aged 91.'

6 Dorothy L. Sayers, *The Mind of the Maker*. London: Methuen, 1941, 104.
7 Sayers, *Mind of the Maker*, 106.
8 Augustine of Hippo, *Confessions*, I.1.1.
9 For Paley's approach, see Alister E. McGrath, *Darwinism and the Divine: Evolutionary Thought and Natural Theology*. Oxford: Wiley-Blackwell, 2011, 85–107.
10 Johann Kepler, *Gesammelte Werke*. Munich: C. H. Beck, 1937–83, vol. 6, 233.

5 Mystery or muddle? The Trinity

1 It is worth noting that the Latin word *creator* actually means 'a male creator'. The idea of 'a female creator' is expressed in Latin using the term *creatrix*.
2 Katharine Farrer (1911–72) authored the 'Inspector Ringwood' trilogy of detective novels, set in Oxford (1952–7).
3 G. K. Chesterton, *St. Francis of Assisi*. London: Hodder & Stoughton, 1923, 16.
4 C. S. Lewis, *The Great Divorce*. London: HarperCollins, 2002, 40.
5 C. S. Lewis, *The Collected Letters of C. S. Lewis*; 3 vols. London: HarperCollins, 2000–6, vol. 2, 145–6.
6 For what follows, see C. S. Lewis, *Mere Christianity*. London: HarperCollins, 2002, 163.
7 Lewis, *Mere Christianity*, 163.
8 'The Poison of Subjectivism', in C. S. Lewis, *Essay Collection*. London: HarperCollins, 2001, 664. Lewis also uses this image in *Mere Christianity*, 162.
9 Gregory of Nazianzus, *Theological Oration*, 41.